THE APPLE
OF HIS EYES

A Spiritual Journey

Chris Scott Ministries

Chris Scott, Chris Scott Ministries

The Apple of His Eyes: A Spiritual Journey

ISBN 978-1-7360211-3-2 (Paperback)
ISBN 978-1-7360211-4-9 (eBook)

Edited by Christine Bode
Book Production by Dawn James, Publish and Promote
Book Cover Design by Trevor Bailey
Design and Layout by Perseus Design

Printed and bound in the United States of America

Note to the reader: The events in this book are based on the writers' memories from their perspectives. Certain names have been changed to protect the identity of those mentioned. The information is provided for educational purposes only. In the event you use any of the information in this book for yourself, which is your constitutional right, the author and publisher assume no responsibility for your actions.

Contents

Introduction

*T*he *Apple of His Eyes: A Spiritual Journey* is a compilation of stories by seven phenomenal women who have accepted the call from God to share their powerful stories. Like David in the Bible, they understand that they are the apple of God's eyes. The co-authors whose hearts will inspire you are Amanda Cohodes, Maja Hodo, Quana Leon, Robyn Rease, Sonya Porter, Sandra James and Toshuna Hanna.

Psalm 17:8 is a prayer of David, prophet and king. David used the phrase "apple of His [God's] eye" in his prayer. "Just as light is reflected on the shiny skin of an apple, and images are reflected in the eyes of a human beholder, God always and constantly let my image be before You and use your power to protect me."

During these challenging times, we need more occasions for self-care and reflection. This book is the perfect volume to curl up with while enjoying a cup or glass of your favorite beverage. Let the stories of these phenomenal ladies inspire you and take you to the next level of your Faith walk. Enjoy!

When I think of these women writers, I am reminded of the following poem by the great Maya Angelou that I dedicate to each of these Queens.

Phenomenal Woman

Pretty women wonder where my secret lies.
I'm not cute or built to suit a fashion model's size
But when I start to tell them,
They think I'm telling lies.
I say,
It's in the reach of my arms,
The span of my hips,
The stride of my step,
The curl of my lips.
I'm a woman
Phenomenally.
Phenomenal woman,
That's me.

I walk into a room
Just as cool as you please,
And to a man,
The fellows stand or
Fall down on their knees.
Then they swarm around me,
A hive of honey bees.
I say,
It's the fire in my eyes,
And the flash of my teeth,
The swing in my waist,
And the joy in my feet.
I'm a woman
Phenomenally.

Phenomenal woman,
That's me.

Men themselves have wondered
What they see in me.
They try so much
But they can't touch
My inner mystery.
When I try to show them,
They say they still can't see.
I say,
It's in the arch of my back,
The sun of my smile,
The ride of my breasts,
The grace of my style.
I'm a woman
Phenomenally.
Phenomenal woman,
That's me.

Now you understand
Just why my head's not bowed.
I don't shout or jump about
Or have to talk real loud.
When you see me passing,
It ought to make you proud.
I say,
It's in the click of my heels,
The bend of my hair,
the palm of my hand,
The need for my care.
'Cause I'm a woman
Phenomenally.

CHAPTER 1

Work the Vision

by Toshuna Hanna

Scripture speaks about faith without works; is death correct? So why do we, as people, think just because we have faith, the vision will come to pass? I know—to wait on the Lord, and He shall renew your strength. The problem is, the Lord has built you up. He has renewed your strength, but you are still waiting on God to move on the vision. You begin to tell yourself you lack energy because the truth is, you do not feel qualified enough to carry the vision.

Strength gives you the fuel that you need to carry out the assignment. As I grow in Christ and the Word, I am unlearning many patterns and behaviors I developed in the past. I have had to rapidly change my mindset because of what the Lord placed in my sight. It was so big that it scared me. At the same time, I wanted it so badly. Have you ever wanted something so badly that you began to change to have it? I would go to work thinking about what I saw. It was so close in my mind that I believed that it would come to pass. However, many of us have a vision and want it now. We live in a microwave society that tells us when we can have anything we want without effort or responsibility. Boy, was I wrong. Work the vision means that I will have the faith to believe that it will come to pass, but I need to be in motion to see results.

In July of 2021, I tested positive for Covid-19. At that moment, I knew I had to fight for my life. I had started to get my foot into the assignment for which God called me. I was walking on the right path. Before I got Covid, I received a vision of death and that I needed to visit my family very soon. So, I booked a flight and headed to Baltimore.

My children and I went to visit my family and friends. Conflicts were mended, relationships strengthened, and some relationships ended. Going home was very sentimental as before then, I had not been home in five years. God graced me for this trip. That visit was much needed.

When I got the test results back, I was devastated. It took my breath away. I called my pastor and his wife, and they comforted me, but honestly, I was so numb all I could think about was my children living without me. At that moment, I felt defeat. It was not until I got on the phone with my mentor, Derashay Zorn, that I heard what I needed to stretch my faith. She said, "What you will experience through this virus is more spiritual than anything you have ever experienced. You must fight it, not in the physical sense, but spiritually, through prayer and reading the Word. I know you are tired but continue because the enemy does not play fair." I heard what she said, and from that day forward, I spoke over my life: *I shall live and not die and declare the works of the Lord.* As God had already given me a future of hope, I knew the vision could not come to pass without me. I am the tool God will use to bring it to fruition.

On the first day I had Covid, I was tired and weak. I tried to continue to record videos and write scripts but was exhausted. By the third day, I had lost my sense of smell and had insomnia; my sleep pattern was so off. That same night, I remember waking up in a panic. As I hallucinated, all I could think was, you will die right here. You did all of this for nothing; now look at you! My entire body felt like it was on fire. I began to yell, and nothing came out.

I got my bible and read the Word. I tried to speak again and said, I shall live and not die and declared the works of the Lord. I repeated that seven times and the last time, I had enough energy to dance. I could feel myself coming back. I received the breakthrough my soul desperately needed.

What bothered me the most was the isolation, loneliness, and helplessness of not being able to move around. What made me fight harder was when the following morning, on Day Four, I opened my door. That whole time my children had to be isolated from each other. I saw my baby girl lying on the floor in front of my room, and it broke me down so badly. I cried like a baby. I began to question how had this happened to me? I was safe! I wore my mask, got the vaccination, and yet there I was with a 103-degree temperature with no energy.

Depression began to kick in, but over and over, I said to myself, I shall live and declare the works of the Lord. I texted my kids and told them to repeat it. We all yelled those words. I SHALL LIVE AND DECLARE THE WORKS OF THE LORD. Over the next couple of days, there was a shift in our house. The dark cloud disappeared; we moved, ate and drank. God healed our bodies.

On Day 14, we went to get tested and still showed positive for Covid. I did not feel sick but had to stay in the house longer. As I look back on these additional 14 days, I prayed and fasted to God about the vision he showed me at the beginning of the year. I said with extreme confidence, Lord, I will live out your will for my life. The scariest thing was the thought of dying with all this anointing in me—with books, business ideas, evangelism, and more. I do not want to make the grave richer when it is my time. I want to die empty, and my legacy shall live on through my children.

I got my fight back. The devil was defeated. His trick did not work, and I am here to testify that you too shall live and not die and declare the works of the Lord. Welcome back to life. Now that you are alive again, it is time to work on the vision.

I developed this concept when I began to see that my goals aligned with my vision, and I began to see progress. Vision gives you faith to believe in the things you see. It comes through dreams, your mind, and what you intuit. For example, I had a vision of being an author. I saw myself speaking in libraries and on different stages about a book with no title. There were many books and many places at which I spoke. Why did I not see it as I had in my vision? Was I supposed to go to where the vision had me in the future?

I needed to get to the stage! I wanted to get to the stage. I knew God gave me the assignment to speak my truth, tell my story, and leave a footprint in the world. This vision kept me up at night. I sat in my bed and prayed. Lord, are you sure you want to use me to speak out to reach the world? How do you want me to do it? I recall His response as clear as day. Write out what you see.

Habakkuk 2:2: "Write the vision and make it plain upon tablets, that he may run that readeth it." We often hear this scripture, but we do not understand it until we have hit rock bottom. Living to survive *is* rock bottom. The only vision you have is to live—and at all costs. It is not until that time that you begin to pray to God for His will to be done in your life. This place is a place of desperation. How desperate are you? Have you tried everything else? Have you tried it your way? Now is the time to live the way God intended you to since before you were born.

Let us unpack this scripture. Once you have a revelation of the scripture, you can work the vision, with confidence.

Write the Vision, Make it Plain

In whatever way you receive the vision, write it down. When you look at it, it may not make sense. But trust me, the pieces will come together. What is it that God has shown you? Was it a business, a book, a promotion, where you started a ministry, marriage, or family? Whatever it may be, write it on paper. You will not receive the entire vision all at once. God gives us snippets of our visions to test our faith. Will you still believe in it even when you cannot see all of it?

Say God gave you the vision that you would be an author as he gave to me. I only saw part of that vision, but I wrote it down and believed it. Yes, I can do this! I love to write. I researched being an author. What does that even look like? I have never written a book before, so I needed to see what that looks like. The definition of vision states, "The ability to think about or plan the future with imagination or wisdom." That is powerful.

Ask yourself this. Can you imagine a future where your life is what God showed you yesterday, last week, or even years ago? Imagine God fulfilling every detail that He revealed to you. I think God himself had a vision when He made the world. After all, He is the creator of all things. God had a vision. He then spoke into existence what He wanted to manifest. God said, "Let there be light," and there was light. So, not only do we have to write the vision, but our language should align with it.

Make It Plain upon Tablets

We must go a little deeper into the vision to understand it after we have it and do our research. Now is the time to write the plan for it. What do you want this vision to accomplish? It can take a long time to put the vision plan into words. Do not beat yourself up about it. Usually, your vision is bound to a passion you have had since childhood. When I was younger, my punishment used to be writing sentences, and I hated it. My hands would ache, and I would be over that assignment. I hated to write the same thing repeatedly, but when I had something in my head, I would write. It did not matter how long I was writing; I would not stop until I finished putting my thoughts on paper to create a story. The most important thing about this story is that telling stories has always been a part of my life. Sometimes we must reflect on where we came from to where we are in the present. You have always had the vision; you did not understand it.

A vision plan ultimately achieves and gives purpose to the existence of an organization, business, ministry, or book. The first book I ever wrote had this vision statement: to help individuals develop a better relationship with God through prayer. Now it is your turn to write out the vision that God has shown you.

So That Others May Run with It

You had a vision and wrote your plan, and now others can run with theirs. A vision statement gives a clear outline of how a business, ministry, or book will come to pass. Identify investors, banks, partners, and staff you want to include. Employers have a vision statement that they display everywhere in their business, on websites and in pamphlets. It lets employees, customers, and partners know what values and characteristics their company possesses. Why does the business exist? It is the same principle that you would get from this verse. Why does your vision exist, and what is its ultimate reason? Through prayer and fasting and staying connected to God, He will begin to reveal those things to us.

In 2018, I created my first vision board. It had all the things that I wanted to happen in my life. When 2019 arrived, and none of the things I put on my vision board had occurred, I was sad. So, in 2019, I added to my vision board and changed some things because I wanted my life to align with the will of God. When I did this, I began to put scripture to what the vision was for my life. At this time, so much was happening; Covid-19 and my aunt passed away from this virus—God rest her soul. I wore many hats and did not know how to navigate each role. I became a teacher, a work-from-home employee, a business owner, and more. My plate was full. It was so full that I had no time for anything else. I thought the pandemic occurred so that we could slow down. I guess it would not slow down for me.

On my TV show, *Living the Victorious Life,* I began to share with my audience of about 40, my vision and what I want for my life. Presently, by the Lord Almighty, those things have come to pass. Not only that, but many of those people also financially supported my vision. I wanted to bless five single mothers for Christmas, and I exceeded that. I knew I had to get my LLC (Limited Liability Company), and out of nowhere, someone handed me an envelope and said, "This is for you to start your business."

What am I saying? It takes courage to write the vision and make it a plan so that others can run with it. Often, it takes trust, faith, and communication. You worry that someone might steal your vision and make it their own. You are not confident enough to appeal for sponsorship, or you simply do not trust that God can use you. Well, I am here to tell you, He can. He will, and He is able.

My Transparent Moment

My mother was told to abort me. I was born three months early, a preemie. I was taken into foster care at ten years old when I suffered the loss of family members and friends. I aged out of the system at 21 and had to live alone as the single mother of a daughter. I did not trust, believe, or walk in God's calling. Death, tragedy, and struggle were what faced me. I was living a life of sin, yet God called me.

In 2013, I lost the love of my life to a senseless murder, and although the way it happened was a tragedy, it was what I needed to move forward. I say that because I was never going to leave Baltimore. It was where I grew up and what I knew. But I left everything I had. People mocked me and said I was making a mistake. Some even said I would die there, but the devil is a liar.

I came to Atlanta with $1500 in my bank account. I still chose to do my own thing. After three years, I found myself in a domestic situation where I almost lost my life. The only thing standing between me and the shotgun was my one-year-old daughter—who I was told to abort. She was my guardian angel that day. Facing all these things, in a small voice, God spoke and said, "That's enough daughter, come home."

Since then, I gave my life to Christ, and walk with Him as His daughter. Jesus has made all the difference. I am healthy, thriving, and on fire for Christ. I can walk into rooms never meant for me to approach. I have made more money than ever before in my life. My business is thriving, and my future looks great. I am internationally recognized and making a global impact. Step out of the boat, Peter, and let Jesus help you. Peter had toiled all night and caught nothing. However, when he allowed Jesus on board, he not only had enough but had to reach out for help because the blessing was that great.

I do not know where you are in your life. Maybe you have faced a similar situation. I want to let you know it is time to live. You have survived. It is time to live in the now. Your assignment is too great to continue walking the path you are on. God has something special for you that your eyes and ears have not seen or heard, but you have received a glimpse. Write it out, pray over it, and at the right time, share it, and watch it manifest into reality. The fact you are still alive is the mere miracle of Jesus Christ. May His glory be a demonstration in your life.

Prayer: Lord, thank you for the vision you placed in my sight. Help my faith move forward in the direction you want my life to go. Help me work on the vision. Give me strength, dedication, and opportunity. Surround me with others who are already where I want to be. I thank you for sight, ears to hear, and a mind that is able and stable. I love you, Jesus, for choosing me to fulfill your will. Thank you for your Word that says that you came, that you might give life, and live more abundantly to those who believe in you. I believe today, and I thank you, Lord, in Jesus' name. Amen.

ABOUT THE AUTHOR

Toshuna Hanna is an ever-evolving woman of character. She dominates her world and encourages those around her. Toshuna published her first book in 2021 called *Pray Until Shift Happens*. She wants the world to have a better relationship with Christ, and what better way than through prayer. Through her coaching program, Look Beyond the Person, Coach Hanna encourages, inspires, and transforms how individuals think, so they are positive and can see the world through another lens. In her newfound position as an entrepreneur, she embraces challenges, welcomes opportunities, and approaches them with a positive attitude.

Toshuna has been internationally recognized by I AM H.E.R International as a Single Mother Nominee of the Year. Her heartfelt passion is to help single mothers worldwide, and she will not stop until her reach becomes impactful.

Toshuna is currently a student finishing her bachelor's degree. She is setting the stage for her three beautiful children to be successful. Unstoppable daughter of God, Toshuna continues to soar with each challenge, knowing that all things are possible and that she will accomplish everything she desires.

CHAPTER 2

Fatherless Daughters

by Sonya (Hill) Porter

As you ride in this metaphorical car as a passenger in my early life's journey, be patient, understanding, and use it to confirm that everyone has a story, and everyone must decide how they will react to the challenges they face. How you contend with your life's journey makes you, YOU.

I am an interesting, intelligent, strong woman of God. I wasn't always this way. I was born to Sandra Webb and John Hill, Jr. in Schenectady, New York, where I lived until I was three years old when my sister was born. I am the oldest of two from my mother and the only child of my father, who died when I was three.

It was a horrible death. He went out with his friends, drinking at a party. His friends took him home and left him on the porch, but they didn't let anybody know that he was there. He was too drunk, and somehow, he choked on his vomit and died. Those friends probably felt horrible their entire adult lives since they abandoned my dad at a time when he should have been able to depend on them.

I used to feel so abandoned because my father passed away and left me. I was angry with God for taking him away from me. Everyone else had their dads, and my mom told me that my dad really loved me. I felt abandoned even though my mother loved me enough for both; there is nothing like having a dad. At least, I would think. I didn't look like my mom. That made it kind of worse. But then again, it made it kind of good. I've so many mixed feelings about everything that has to do with my father. Why didn't my father's family look for me? Why did we leave and never go back? Who are my family members? Where did I come from? I don't look like my mom, so do I look like my dad's family? I only have two pictures of my dad. How sad is that?

Let me tell you about my journey without my dad. My mother and I share a fatherless life. Her father was absent although alive. He had a hard life, to say the least; he left home at 14 and began hustling to survive. He got my grandmother pregnant when he was only 19, and she was 18. What did he know about raising kids? Nothing, he had to hustle for everything he got, and he wasn't consistent in their lives.

My mother raised my sister and me with love, security, and courage. Each of us makes decisions based on many things, and my family was no different. I thank God for every experience throughout my life, and for allowing me to share some of them with you. I wouldn't change a thing. However, history can repeat itself unless we make changes.

After my father passed away, his mother wanted my mother to allow her to raise me. When my mother said no, my grandmother tried to pressure her, so my mother moved and never returned to New York. That's why I never knew any of my dad's side of the family. I recently met four of my first cousins on my dad's side, thanks to my sister's diligent work in searching for them. I was able to obtain several pictures and I can see where I came from. That is awesome. My cousins welcomed and accepted me immediately. The timing was perfect for all of us.

Mom is a wonderful woman, very independent, but deeply religious in the Muslim faith. For my mom, marriage was necessary—a requirement within the religion; if one marriage didn't work, you married repeatedly until you got it right. She believed that children needed a father figure to help in their growth and development.

I grew up with two stepfathers, and my sister had three stepfathers. My sister is almost three years younger than me, and she looked up to me more than I knew. My first stepfather lived with us in Springfield, Massachusetts. He was wonderful and brought along a wonderful family that I love to this day. We lived in a two-family flat with a basement. We went to public school; our house was the second house from the corner and lucky for us, the bus stop was right there. This was the same place where I had my first fight. I was only eight years old, and a boy wanted to fight my sister because she disagreed with his little sister, and I wasn't having it, so I beat him up. Our sisters remained friends until we moved, but he and I didn't speak anymore.

I remember when I was about six and my little sister was three, a friend of my mother lived with us on the weekends while she attended college. She was driving us to an outing in my mom's old blue Chevy when we were struck by another vehicle. I was so scared. There weren't any cell phones back then, so I ran home, which wasn't too far, to get my mom. I started stuttering because of my fear about the accident, so my mom had to be calm to help me relax enough to tell her what happened. She knew there was a problem when I walked home alone, but once I was able to explain what was happening, she contacted the authorities. Mom expressed to me how proud she was of how I handled a serious situation. Although the car was totaled, there were no severe injuries. That is when my sister started looking up to me, and I became the protector of the family.

When we moved from Massachusetts, it happened abruptly. My mother woke us up in the middle of the night whispering, "Get up and move quickly and quietly," as she took us down to the basement of our two-story family flat with only trash bags carrying all our things. She put us into the car, and off we went. No warning. No conversation. Just off to a new life. This was traumatic for us as the friends we once knew were gone, and my stepfather didn't come with us. We never went back. At the time, we didn't know what was happening and when I asked my mom, she said, "Just go to sleep; it will all be OK." So, I did.

When I woke, we had moved to Ypsilanti, Michigan. At this point, I was about nine years old, and my sister was six. We moved in with my aunt and cousins who lived right around the corner from my grandmother. That made the transition bearable, even though I didn't know them very well. They had moved there from Schenectady. My cousin and I became remarkably close, and I made some good lifelong friends. Life began to get back to normal. Shortly after we moved there, we got a three-bedroom townhouse in the same apartment complex, which was exciting because I started feeling more secure with where we lived.

Sometime later, my stepfather arrived, and our family thrived. I was enjoying life. I loved living there. I had my first peck on the lips, a few more fights, and experienced death for the first time when my great uncle died. I was so hurt by his death. I knew he wasn't doing very well, but nobody took me seriously because he downplayed his sickness, and he died the next day. My grandmother, his sister, couldn't go back into her house as he died sitting at her kitchen table. She was out of town at her mother's funeral when he died, and when she returned, she moved into a high-rise for seniors. She was also upset because my great uncle was buried with her dentures, so she had to buy new ones. Even with all this going on, I was there with my family and friends, so life was great.

My stepfather was good to my sister and me, but what I didn't know is that he wasn't always good to my mom. The first time I saw them fighting, my stepfather had my mom pinned down, partially on the bed, with her feet hanging, barely touching the floor. She was yelling and struggling to get up. I couldn't understand why he was holding her down. When I yelled at him, he looked at me, which allowed her to grab the telephone sitting on the headboard behind her and hit him in the head. He told me to go to my room, and my mom was able to get away from him. I was so scared that I could hardly breathe. My heart was pounding, I was crying, and all I could do was lay in my bed and rock until I fell asleep. Sometime later, my mom made him move out, which made me sad too, because he was the only father that I knew, and I loved his whole family. I never saw him again. He abandoned me. Two fathers were gone.

We continued to live there, and it was time for me to start middle school. I was so excited to join my cousin, but my mom had different plans. She decided that we needed to move to Inkster, Michigan, which was about 30 minutes from where we were living, and I had to change schools from a public school to a Muslim school. This was a shock. No warning, no conversation, just another traumatic move, leaving family and friends behind.

I didn't know anyone in my new neighborhood. A van would pick us up and take us to Detroit for school along with other kids that lived in Inkster. My sister and I didn't have a choice in going to Sister Clara Muhmmad School, but she adapted way better than I did, possibly because she was younger, and she was able to remain at the same school as I was attending. We had to wear a uniform; long oversized skirts that touched the ground with long oversized sleeveless tops that stopped close to our knees, white long-sleeved shirts under our tops, and scarves covering our heads. We wore this uniform no matter what the season. I was so embarrassed about wearing the uniform even though I didn't have any friends in the neighborhood. I didn't want anyone outside of the school to see me; I hated being different. I hated for people to stare at me, so I would wear a pair of jeans under my skirt so that I could pull my uniform skirt up and put it all under a jacket so that the only thing that was showing was my jeans and a jacket, with a hood or hat so that you wouldn't know I was wearing a head scarf. I didn't believe in what the Muslim culture represented, what they taught, nor did I agree with their treatment of women. I wanted nothing to do with them. My mother became a Muslim when I was about three years old as she made her move to Massachusetts, even though she was raised as a Christian. To this day my mother and sister are both Muslims.

My school didn't look like a normal school. It was a small, two-story building with classrooms on both levels, with a large open room for praying and gathering when they wanted everyone together. When I started my new school, I was terribly angry and had become depressed, even though I made a few friends. I was very rude, disrespectful, mean, argumentative, and aggressive because I didn't care.

I no longer wanted to live after too many abrupt moves and too much change. I couldn't bear it anymore, so I took a bottle of pills, believing that it would be over soon. Only it wasn't. I woke up madder than I was the night before. What happened? How was I alive? Why didn't God want me? He left me alone to stay there and suffer. My third father was gone. I thought that Jesus Christ didn't want to be bothered with me either. I recalled my father's death as he had left me in the world, alone with no protection.

My behavior became worse. No one could tell me what to do and when they tried, I would do the opposite. I was a complete hot mess. My mother never knew that I was that depressed. I don't think it would have resulted in me changing schools, but I do think she would have tried to comfort me and talk me through being there, which wouldn't have helped me at all. Only one friend knew that I had taken the pills, and she was scared until she saw me at school the next day. I'm not sure why none of the teachers told my mother about my behavior. She wouldn't have tolerated it. They thought it was a temporary situation and that

I would grow out of it. I didn't. Several of my friends left the school, which housed first-graders to twelfth-graders, one classroom per grade.

During the summer we had to go to a Muslim camp which I hated, although it was only for a week. I don't remember whose idea it was, but a few girls, including me, decided that we didn't like this one girl, so we were going to make it look like she had urinated on herself during the night. One of the girls urinated in a coke can and another girl poured it on her and the bed, but she woke up and saw us standing there and told on us. I was the only one that got into trouble. The camp counselor said that I had to have been the ringleader even though I didn't pour the pee on her. I had to write an apology letter to her and read it to the entire camp, admitting guilt. You would think that I would have been embarrassed, but I wasn't I didn't even care. I was a leader at an early age, although I didn't know it. I was leading in the wrong direction, but I was leading.

In Eighth Grade, I got in trouble in school but not as much as in Seventh Grade. I had calmed down a bit, until closer to the end of the year when the principal decided he was going to punish me for unruly behavior. Normally, the staff would have the entire school enter the praying hall, and they would paddle you in front of everyone. They did that often— it didn't matter if you were a boy or girl, a man would paddle you—but he knew that wasn't going to fly with me, so he took a different approach. He told me to go sit in the Fourth-Grade classroom to do my work, thinking this punishment would embarrass me into behaving. I wasn't embarrassed, but I was tired of fighting the world. So, for once, I did as I was told. I went to the classroom, completed the work, and attempted to turn the work in the following day to the principal.

When I arrived at school the next day, I followed the principal's instructions and brought my work to his office to be checked so that I could go back to my classroom. The assistant principal was there but the principal was not. I showed my work to the assistant principal, and he told me I could return to class. About an hour later, the principal realized that I was back in class, and he came to that class to try to embarrass me again, instructing me to go back to the Fourth-Grade class, but I refused. I refused because although I did what I was told, he wanted to continue to punish me unnecessarily. The staff took pride in embarrassing kids. They thought this would motivate us to not misbehave, but it didn't work with me. As we argued about my going back to the Fourth-Grade class, he wouldn't allow me to call my mom, so the secretary snuck out and called her. He was screaming at me, threatening me, and I was doing the same to him. My mom could hear the ruckus over the phone and rushed over to the school to find complete chaos.

Mom followed the principal around the school, trying to find out what was going on, and he kept ignoring her and walking off while she was talking. Muslim women didn't have a voice, and especially divorced women with two kids could not question the authority of the principal. To avoid her, he went into the boy's bathroom thinking she wouldn't follow him, but she did. The fear of a man hitting my mom again surfaced, and I retrieved a knife from a friend at school and went into the bathroom where they were. I started threatening the principal with the knife, which shocked my mother because no one had ever told her about my behavior. She had always thought that I was an excellent, well-behaved child, as I was at home. We left, and I was expelled from school. My mom removed my sister from that school as well.

I was free, but I had to go through another change. I thought we were going to move back to Ypsilanti, where I would go to school with my cousins, but that was not the case. My mom always tried to do what was best for us, so we started going to Romulus Middle School with only a month of school left. She took us to that school until she found an apartment, and we moved again. Starting a new school was a little stressful, but I was so relieved to be out of the Muslim school.

Living in Romulus was great. I went to high school, played sports, experienced my first love, had friends—of course, got into a fight—but everything was wonderful until my mom re-married a man with two boys that were younger than us. Then it happened again. We moved to St. Louis, Missouri, because my new stepfather was being transferred. I begged my mom to let me live with my grandmother, but she said no, that I was her responsibility, and she would be the one to raise me. Sad, once again, because of another move, she allowed me to stay in Michigan over the summer with my best friend (at the time) and her family until school started and then I had to go to Missouri. That was the best summer ever. There is always some good to be found, even in bad situations.

Life in Missouri for the first six months was tough. We had to pay for long-distance calls, so my first love and I would write letters, and I would sign them with a kiss using some of my mother's lipstick. Eventually, we faded out. I joined the basketball team, started making friends, and fell in love again. St. Louis wasn't a bad place. I went to a good school and lived in a nice house, but things started to change when my stepfather became abusive to my mother.

One day I walked in on my stepfather sitting on top of my mother as she lay on the floor in the living room. He was holding her down with her hands above her head, and she was struggling to get up, calling out for help. I launched into attack mode and started swinging on him till he got off my mother, and then I ran out of the house and across the street to a girlfriend's house and stayed there. When I talked to my mom, she told me to stay there until everything cooled off, which was only for the rest of the day. However, when I looked outside, I saw that he had thrown all my things outdoors, but before I went home, Mom took everything and put it back in my room.

The way my room was set up was great because I had the entire basement to myself. There was my bedroom, a connecting bathroom, the laundry room, and a huge living room with glass doors that opened to a fenced-in backyard where we had a dog named Bullet. I loved it.

My stepfather might have been trying to do the right thing when he tried to give my sister a whooping, but it didn't sit well with me. She screamed as you do when you're being hit with a belt; I attacked. I swung at him, hit him, grabbed the belt, and hit him with it. Then, of course, I ran and called my mom from my friend's house. Mom told me to stay over there until she got home from work, and she'd deal with it when she got there.

Each time, my mom would smooth everything over with everybody, and we would move forward. You must remember that I always felt like I had to be the protector of the family, and I would do just that. I wasn't a perfect child like my mom thought, but I was very loving and respectful to most people. I wasn't disrespectful in any other school except for Muslim school, even though I used to fight a whole lot, especially when I was in Michigan.

One night, I was in my room in the basement when I was awakened by banging and yelling upstairs. My heart started pounding, fear kicked in again, and it sounded worse than any other incident. I ran up the ten stairs to find my mother and stepfather arguing and tussling. As she ran out the door into the garage to get in my gray Ford Fusion to get away from him, he followed her, grabbed a baseball bat that was sitting by the door in the carport, and bust out the driver's side window as she tried to flee. I ran to the kitchen drawer. He could see me through the glass door and was right on my tail, Mom coming behind him. I grabbed the largest butcher knife I could find in those quick moments and turned toward him yelling, as I threatened to kill him. Time seemed as if it was moving so slowly, yet everything happened at warp speed. I genuinely wanted to kill him and would have, if a big burly white police officer hadn't come in the door. The officer observed me threatening my stepfather and told me to put the knife down, in an extremely calm voice. I told him I couldn't put the knife down because I had to kill him. The police officer guaranteed me that if I put the knife down, he would take care of the situation for me. My mom begged me to put the knife down. As I put it down, my stepfather ran through the house out the front door, jumped in his station wagon, and sped off up the street. The police officer chased him on foot and then by car.

That was a pivotal moment in my life. At that point, I decided that I wanted to be a cop. And that I wanted to be the protector of those suffering from domestic violence.

I graduated from high school and returned to Michigan that summer until I left to go to the Marine Corps. Many people asked why I chose the Marine Corps, and I told them the Marine Corps chose me. While at the mall one Saturday afternoon, I noticed a Black female and male walking around in a uniform, and I thought to myself, I want to do whatever it is the two of them do because they looked amazing in their uniforms. They exuded success. I approached them and inquired, and they happened to be Marine recruiters. They came to the house to talk to my mom, and even though she was surprised that I wanted to join, she agreed. I called my cousin who was still in Michigan and asked her to join with me. She agreed, and we both joined on October 27, 1986.

All I know is that God had my back even when I didn't believe that He did. Every aspect of my life was important as it made me who I am. Every experience, good and bad, was a part of my journey. We always think that clichés like "after heartache comes ease" don't mean anything, but they are so right. Most clichés come from people who have experienced something major and made it through. I also had a praying mother. No matter her religion, she believed in God, and she instilled in me that He is always sitting next to me. When times are hard, it is difficult to feel God's presence.

Maybe if I had allowed myself to cry, I would have been less emotionally restricted. When I felt the need to cry, I would give myself a certain amount of time, such as ten minutes, and I would time myself. I would let loose for only that amount of time, and then I would shut it off, and I didn't allow myself to cry about that issue again. I wasn't taught to be this way; my mom and sister cry all the time. For me, this was the only way I could be the protector of my family. How unhealthy! Now I have all these emotions boxed up, sitting on the shelf in my heart with nowhere to go. I fear opening these boxes because I don't know what will come out. Am I over my past?

God made me tough so I could perform at another level in life. My childhood was good—I had some great times—and I choose to focus more on the good times than the bad.

My mom focused on making sure that she provided a safe, secure, and loving environment for her girls, and she did just that. I'm proud that my mother didn't keep us in an abusive situation. When things turned sour, she left the relationship to protect us and herself. She was always very affectionate and made decisions based on our needs. If she had financial struggles, we didn't know about it. I never had to worry about if we had enough food to eat. My mother never knew that I felt like I had to be the family protector. Like so many of us, my mom had terrible taste in men. In her defense, her father and grandfather were not good role models.

No one has a perfect childhood. Parenting is a trial-and-error experiment, and each child is different, each experience perceived differently. How you deal with hardship is what separates you from others. It hasn't always been easy, but if you look at life like everything comes down to how you choose to react to harsh conditions, it can change your life forever. For example, with something as small as when someone cuts you off in traffic, choose not to get upset. Allow them grace, send them blessings, and see how it makes you feel. It has made a substantial difference in my life.

Growing up, even though my childhood was a roller-coaster ride, I didn't always feel that life was great. Sometimes I felt like life was pretty F****D up. However, I learned how to master living life in fight or flight mode, which helped me in my career choices as an adult. It helped me with my 4 years is the Marine Corps, and I fulfilled my dream of becoming a police officer and served my community for over 25 years. My cousin retired from the Marine Corps after 20 years. We are still the best of friends.

What would I tell my younger self, now that I'm 53? Self, everything that you're going through is all for your own good. You're not going to understand that. But you must ride it out. When you think about the pain that you're experiencing in relationships, friendships, and even in work-ships, each thing will prepare you for something else. So, always hold your head up high and have no regrets. Every decision that you make is the right decision at that time. Every time you do something, you will learn something. Give yourself a break. Know that nothing is perfect, not your body, mind, soul, or your heart. Sometimes, I want you to just laugh at yourself and learn to enjoy the journey. Most of us want to plan every moment of every day, every week, every year. Life really doesn't work that way. Don't get me wrong, we must make plans and set goals. Just don't let it consume you, and don't be so hard on yourself when your plans don't go the way you want them to! Look at life like every decision is a left turn and continue making left turns to add different experiences to your journey.

I had a boyfriend that I loved. He looked like Malcolm X, and I thought he was gorgeous. I thought we were meant to be together. That was not the case. Or maybe it was the case for that season. During that season, he taught me how not to love myself. He made me feel as if my body was ugly. Even though, as years passed, other men would say how beautiful I was, I could never get past the fact that he thought that I wasn't beautiful. You might be saying to yourself, "Oh, that wouldn't happen to me. I'm too confident. My mom told me I was beautiful my whole life." Well, it can happen to you. My experience with that man lowered my self-esteem, although I was exceptionally good at pretending to be confident when I wasn't. He undermined my confidence in personal relationships and my femininity. However, he probably also helped me to not become promiscuous. Now that I'm in my fifties, I have changed the way I see myself, the way I see others, and the way that I love. It's the weirdest thing. Don't waste all the time that I did.

Assess yourself, and if you realize that you are a natural-born leader, accept that. If it's not natural and you want to be a leader, become one. Always use your talents in a positive way and continue to help others. Even though you can't choose every situation in your life, you can choose how you respond. You get to choose how you handle situations that are out of your control, to get up every day and to lean on a higher power.

When I was a teenager, I decided that the Muslim religion wasn't for me. I didn't believe that men should suppress women; yes, we are helpmates to men, but not their slaves. Women bring value to this world, and not only through bearing and raising children. My experiences with the Muslim religion were negative, so I started reading the Bible to get a better understanding of Christ. I'm still growing in my walk with God and I pray that he continues to guide my steps.

As I looked back at my life, I realized that God has been with me all along, even when I was mad at him. God never said that you won't go through anything, he said he would be there with you. God is always sitting next to you. Treat Him like he's your best friend. Talk to Him and listen to Him. You are not alone. Be the change agent in your life. Be blessed. You are so loved.

Writing this chapter was hard. It made me look at myself and why I might have made so many of the decisions that I did. I may not be the sort of God-fearing woman who can read off scriptures for every situation, but I am loved by my creator and that is wonderful to me. He protected me during my career as a police officer and carried me through the ranks to become an assistant chief at a large metropolitan agency. Believe me, it wasn't easy working in a white male-dominated field. I had to pull from the strength of God many times to continue over 25 years with the department and over 30 years in law enforcement. During that time, I married and had children. I thank God that my children had a dependable and present father/stepfather even though we divorced after 13 years of marriage. Many years later, I found love again and plan to marry an amazing man. God told me on a mission trip that he was going to be my husband, and it is happening. This has reconfirmed for me that God really does have my back, always. I am retired now and continue to do God's work.

Love yourself. I have to say that again. LOVE YOURSELF. Don't let anybody take loving yourself away from you. And remember, God loves you too. Be blessed.

STAND ON HIS WORD

ABOUT THE AUTHOR

 Sonya Porter is a retired Assistant Chief of the DeKalb County Police Department. She served her community as a law enforcement professional for over 30 years. Sonya served her country as a Corporal in the United States Marine Corps. She holds a bachelor's degree in Criminal Justice from Saint Leo University and a Master of Science degree in Public Administration from Troy University. She is an entrepreneur and co-owns two thriving businesses, T & T Bakery and The Rose @BayRose Air BNB. Sonya is a Certified Professional Life Coach specializing in Leadership. She has taken her military and police officer training in Leadership and translated it into pursuing her passion of helping people live their best lives.

Sonya is the proud mother of Tamika, Tamia and son-in-law Kenny, Michael, and bonus son, Jordan. Tyler, her grandson, is the light of her life. She is a local and global missionary. Sonya has served in Belize, South Africa, Costa Rica and within the United States. When not on the mission field or spending time with family, she loves empowering young adults as a basketball coach.

CHAPTER 3

Lost but Not Alone

by Maja Hodo

I was wearing my pretty pink lace-covered dress with frilly socks to match, and black patent leather shoes. Mom had done my hair in ponytails with ribbons, and it looked sweet. While playing on the steps in the hallway of one of my mom's friend's apartment complexes, her older son came over and began to tell me how pretty I looked as he sat down on the steps to watch me play. He called me to come over to where he was sitting so, he could see how lovely I looked in my dress. Reluctantly, I moved forward to where he was, and as I got closer, he pulled me onto his lap. As he continued to express how nice he thought I looked in my cheerful pink lacey dress, he opened my legs and began to touch and rub me in my private area.

At first, he touched me on the outside of my panties underneath my dress, but as he continued, I felt his hand move to the inside of my panties. I was so afraid and confused about what he was doing to me. I sat on his lap with my hands in my mouth— terrified—with tears in my eyes while he told me how pretty I looked, thinking that what he was doing to me was all my fault because I was pretty. Those words negatively connected to me as he touched me. I felt dirty and nasty, and like it was my fault that this happened to me because I was pretty. I started to hate and blame myself for what he did.

I was too young, maybe three or four years old at the time, to realize what was going on, but I remember feeling utterly and completely shattered. As my mom and her friend came out of the apartment, he quickly sat me down on the step next to him, telling me to be quiet. He wasn't telling me to be quiet because I had tears in my eyes but because he didn't want me to tell. This traumatic event was the first of many memories I have which affected the way that I saw myself as I grew older. I never told anyone what happened to me that day in the hallway in my pretty pink lace-covered dress, not even my mom.

Over time, I managed to store this traumatic event in the back of the deepest, darkest part of my mind. Out of sight out of mind, right? Well, I was wrong because being molested at an incredibly young age drastically changed my life. Those words he said, "You look so PRETTY!" were always in the back of my mind, and growing up, when people told me that I was pretty or cute, I would cringe. I equated being pretty with being molested, and I hated hearing people tell me how pretty I was. I became very introverted and kept to myself a lot after that event. I didn't like for my mom to dress me often in dresses, especially ones with a lot of lace or that were pink. I became a tomboy so that I wouldn't look too feminine, and I would play with my brother and his friends a lot so that I could be seen as one of the boys. Anything that brought attention to me or that made me stand out, I tried to avoid because I didn't want to be seen. I didn't want to be recognized or regarded as pretty.

This incident was Satan's first attack on my self-esteem. As the years went by and I got older, during my primary age, I experienced many other attacks that sabotaged my self-worth. My father and mother were in and out of my life due to their drug and alcohol addictions, but thanks be to God, they overcame their addictions. I desperately sought to fill a void that was created unintentionally by my parents when I was a child. Even though they conquered their demons, I was still left with a void. I thought something was wrong with me because, when I was young, I didn't realize or understand why my parents chose other things over me. I didn't understand or have anyone to help me understand that they were dealing with things that had absolutely nothing to do with me.

I felt utterly rejected because of the lack of a relationship with my father while growing up. I recall an incident when my dad was supposed to pick me up to spend the day with him. I can't remember how old I was, but I wasn't old enough to tell time. I only knew the difference between day and night. My father called saying that he was coming to get my brother and me, and I remember feeling super excited because we rarely saw him. I got up early that morning, washed my face, brushed my teeth, and made sure that Mom did my hair. She styled my hair in big thick ponytails with white bows on them. I got dressed in a cute shirt and jeans and waited in the living room on the sofa by the screen door, so I could see him when he arrived.

The feeling that I had while waiting on that sofa by the door was like Christmas Day. Every time a car drove by, I jumped up and rushed to the door thinking it was my dad, but it wasn't. Dad was so infrequently involved in my life that I had no idea what his car looked like. I waited and waited by that door looking out of it until it got dark outside. Once it was dark, I knew he wasn't coming. I was devastated and crushed. He never showed up—no phone call, nothing. My heart was broken in two, and I felt so rejected. Brokenhearted, I shed so many tears that I cried myself to sleep that night. Sadly, many more of these events occurred throughout my childhood. Every time this happened, it brought back the feeling that something was wrong with me. Something had to be wrong if my father didn't want to spend time with me. His rejection added to the low self-esteem and self-worth that I already had from being molested.

A few years later, there came a time when my brother and I had to live with my dad and stepmom because Mom was in rehab. While staying with them, I witnessed another side of my dad that was physically and verbally abusive to my stepmom. There were nights when we were asleep and Dad came home drunk and jumped on my stepmom, punching and beating her, waking us all. She had done nothing to deserve what he did to her.

My stepmom was a saved woman and the first person in my life to introduce me to Christ. She was loving, gentle, soft-spoken and would do anything for us. She couldn't have children, but she loved my brother and me like we were her own. After everything my dad did to her, she never said a mean word or treated him with hatred. It was through her that I first witnessed Christ.

She would get my brother and me and walk us down the street to a church that stayed open to the public. She walked with us, holding our hands until we reached the church. Then she would sit down on one of the benches, and weep and pray. My step-mom did this often, especially after Dad, in one of his drunken stupors, decided to beat her for the demons he carried. She never raised a hand to hit him back, only to protect herself from the blows that he delivered. She never retaliated or called the police on him to arrest him for beating her either. Instead, she would just take my brother and me to that little church down the street and pray. She prayed for my dad and his deliverance. Seeing her do these things became a crucial part of my healing process that took place later in my life.

Watching my stepmom turn to Christ after each altercation she had with my dad was instrumental in my acceptance of Christ at an early age. I didn't do this at a church while being prayed for, laying at the altar, or even in the presence of my stepmother. My moment of salvation came one day while I was playing hide and seek outside with my brother and some of our friends. Amid running to find a place to hide, I heard a voice clearly say to me, "I have more for you." When I heard it, I stopped clear in my tracks which was something I tried to do from the time I was molested. And I answered yes. At that moment, I had no clue who or what I had heard say those words to me, but I knew it was an opportunity I could not reject.

I wanted "the more" that I heard the voice of God say that He had for me. My young life had already been full of trials and tribulations, so I knew I had to say yes to that voice. Once I said yes out loud, I immediately felt peace, as if the sun itself was embracing me at that very moment. I felt loved for the first time in my life.

Don't think that just because I said yes to God and gave my life to Christ that everything was made right from that day forth—because it wasn't. After that day of playing hide and seek, I experienced more trauma, trials and tribulations, and that feeling of being rejected and not being wanted or loved, returned time and time again. Although I gave my life to Christ in my youth, I had no one to show me how to develop my relationship with God. I only stayed with my dad and stepmom for a few months. I saw my stepmom praying, but she never taught me what prayer was, what it meant to develop a relationship with God, or how important it was to do so once you gave your life to Christ. After receiving salvation, I still had trouble accepting myself. I couldn't get past the memory of what happened to me as a child, and I couldn't get over the memories of my inconsistent parents. I struggled with liking myself, and I let anything and everything that people had to say about me, take root in my mind. As I got older and the years passed, I took any kind of rejection as evidence that something was wrong with me. If I couldn't make friends in school, I believed something was wrong with me, and I wasn't worthy of friendships. I did things to make people like me so that I could be their friend. I compromised who I was to make friends, but I was miserable. I tried to fit in where I didn't fit. I tried to be someone I wasn't.

The first relationship I had was in high school, and to keep that relationship, I compromised a lot. I lost my virginity even though I wasn't ready to. I made a fool of myself on several occasions, trying to be a part of the "in-crowd." At one point, when the relationship ended, I begged him not to leave me. I was devastated when it seemed like he moved on to another relationship so easily. My self-esteem was so low at that point that I still let him in even though I knew he was involved with someone else. I was a complete fool about this person just because I didn't want to be alone. I repeated the same pattern when I went to college.

Through everything that I experienced, I could always hear that voice in the back of my mind saying, "I have more for you." So, on top of how I felt about myself, hearing that voice in the back of my mind added conviction. It made me feel so bad I would sink into depression. I didn't know what to do about it, but I knew I was tired of feeling that way. On many occasions, I considered suicide. I thought of ways to kill myself and even wrote letters in my journal for my mom to find once I had committed the act. But that voice would always stop me from carrying it out. I was tired—tired of having suicidal thoughts, tired of not feeling good enough, tired of repeating in my head the negative words that had been spoken to me repeatedly through the years—and I decided to turn to God.

At this point in my life, I went faithfully to church. I had received the gift of the Holy Spirit but was still trying to hide. I didn't want people to see the many flaws I thought I had. I was still that little girl playing hide and seek, running to find a place to hide on the inside. I had to heal from the wound I suffered as a child. I had to face my fears, the truths and untruths about myself. I had to do the unbearable thing that I had become so good at avoiding, which was to face myself. I was lost and had no clue as to who I was. I allowed people to tell me who I was and who I wasn't, but I wanted to know who God said I was. I realized and admitted to myself that I was broken.

The journey of finding myself while being broken wasn't an easy task or a fast process. To heal from my brokenness, I knew I had to turn to the one person that knew me better than I knew myself. I had to turn to God. In Isaiah 26:3, the Bible tells us, "You will keep *him* in perfect peace, whose mind is stayed on You, because he trusts in You." (NKJV)

My mind was scattered and God was in the far back portion of it. Even though I was going to church every Sunday, hearing the Word of God, I still felt horrible on the inside because all I could focus on were negative thoughts. I constantly looked up scriptures in the Bible to help me heal from a spirit of rejection. I had good days and not-so-good days, and some horrible days where I just wanted to give up. It sounds easy, but it wasn't easy at all. Sitting down with myself was one of the hardest things I have ever had to do. There were nights when I would cry myself to sleep holding my pillow. At times, I felt like God wasn't there with me during what I was going through, and depression would try to creep back in. There were also times when I experienced feelings of overwhelming happiness. God was there with me, I was on cloud nine, and there wasn't anything in the whole wide world that could bring me down. The process of healing wasn't easy, but I knew deep down inside that I was worth it. I deserved it, and so do YOU!!

After praying, fasting, and studying the Bible, that little voice inside still fed me negativity. One way I conquered it and something I still do, is to surround myself with what God says about me. In my prayer and study time, I read the thoughts that He has towards me. At times it was still hard for me to believe once I'd read them, so I decided to get index cards to write every positive word (scripture) that God said concerning me. I put one on my mirror telling me how beautiful God thought I was, which said, "I will praise You, for I am fearfully and wonderfully made; Marvelous are Your works, and *that* my soul knows very well."

(Psalm 139:14) On my refrigerator was an index card that said, "And my God shall supply all your need according to His riches in glory by Christ Jesus" (Philippians 4:19) which reassured me that there would never be a time when He wouldn't take care of me. On the medicine cabinet in my bathroom, I posted Isaiah 53:5, which declares, "But he *was* wounded for our transgressions, *he was* bruised for our iniquities; The chastisement of our peace *was* upon Him; And by His stripes we are healed." I placed different scriptures around my house to remind me of the positive thoughts and feelings that God has towards me.

By doing this, I changed the way I saw and felt about myself. I changed my perception of myself to God's perception of me, and who He called me to be. By spending time with God through scripture and prayer, I am fine with not being accepted by everyone. I got to know who I am as a person, a woman, and a Christian. Whenever I found myself returning to a place of "woe is me," I turned to prayer. I turned to God. I knew that He would understand exactly what I was feeling and would be able to help me release it. "My frame was not hidden from You, When I was made in secret, *and* skillfully wrought in the lowest parts of the earth. Your eyes saw my substance, being yet unformed. And in Your book, they all were written, the days fashioned for me, when *as yet there were* none of them." (Psalm 139:15-16) I realized that no one knew me better than God. After all, He created me.

The more that I prayed and read my Bible, I realized that I worried less. My thoughts of suicide disappeared, anxiety left me, and my fear of everything was gone. I loved the person that I was and was becoming. I was mentally transformed and renewed in my mind (Romans 12:2). The more I turned to God, I realized I was finding myself. I am more than just a person who was molested as a child, I am an overcomer. When I felt rejected and unloved because of absent parents in my childhood, I realized that I am loved unconditionally and was never alone with God. John 15:5-8 (MSG) says perfectly what I experienced at this moment in my life. I realized that I was nothing without God and that everything I needed to be healed from brokenness and set free from a spirit of rejection was found in Him. I was in my mid to late twenties when I was delivered from these things. It is not too late for God to move on your behalf and in your situation.

I surround myself with the Word of God and take comfort in prayer and communicating with Him whenever I am going through a rough time. I lean on Him in my weakest moments because even though I am delivered from the things that held me mentally bound, the enemy will often try to move against me. The difference this time is that I am assured that God is with me, and I have His word to fight with. I finally understand the "more" that He had for me when I first heard His voice.

My life isn't without problems or tough times. I still experience challenges and there are times when Satan tries to make me think that God doesn't care about me or the things I experience. The difference now is that I know exactly who I am to God. Through spending time in prayer and with His Word, I know what my purpose is. I embrace myself, flaws and all.

I have done the one thing that I never thought I could. I forgave the person that molested me and forgave my father for not being there for me. I knew I forgave them because when I encountered them, the feelings I once had no longer existed. Instead, I felt compassion for them, and I prayed for them. I also realized that forgiving them wasn't for them, it was for me, and it was why I was able to heal completely. Once I forgave them, they no longer controlled me, my thoughts, emotions, or actions. Through forgiveness, I was no longer afraid to talk about my feelings, especially when it came time to tell my mother about her friend's son molesting me in the hallway. I could talk about what happened to me that day and how it broke me. I could open up to other women who were molested as children and help them to understand that what happened to them was not their fault or due to anything that they'd done wrong. I was no longer embarrassed by my beauty and the way God created me. I was able to embrace it.

When it came to my dad, I had to wait until he dealt with his demons to be able to sit down and talk to him. Once I had that opportunity, I openly expressed my forgiveness. I still only see him about once a year, around Christmas. It's ironic because those times that I waited, excited for him to come, felt like Christmas to me, and now I see him only at Christmas when he comes to bring my children their gifts. Each year when I see him, I make sure he knows how much I love him because I no longer hold him responsible for not being there for me. When I forgave him, I broke the chain of bondage that kept me from getting to where God wanted me to be, in Him.

The freedom that I found in Christ is the reason that I can write about this small portion of my life's journey and share it with you. My purpose in Christ set me free. I realize that with most people I encounter, their greatest struggle is to figure out what ministry God is calling them to. I possess profound compassion for helping other young girls and women to find their worth in Christ. I desire to be the person I needed when I was a little girl, for those of this generation, because I didn't have anyone to talk to or confide in when I was going through significant challenges. I want young girls and women all over the world to see themselves through the eyes of God.

A Personal Message from Maja

Dear Heavenly Father,

I thank You for the beautiful woman holding this book. Lord, I pray that as she reads every word written, she hears Your voice and feels Your heart of compassion and unconditional love that You have for her. Father, I decree and declare that as she reads this book from beginning to end that healing within her will occur. I pray that You will renew the mind of this beautiful woman. Transform the way that she thinks and the way that she sees herself. I pray that the scales that have been covering her eyes will fall off and she will see herself through Your eyes, Lord! Give her the understanding that You desire to have intimate time alone with her, to equip and prepare her so that she can be everything that You have created her to be. Lord, soften her heart so that she will be able to forgive those that hurt her and abused her, just as you forgive us, and fill her with Your compassion and unconditional love. Father, I decree and declare that the chains of bondage that have been holding her bound will be loosed in Jesus' name! I decree and declare in the name of Jesus that every word curse that has ever been spoken against her in her life is broken now! I establish by the power of the Holy Spirit that this is her moment of freedom, and she will be victorious, in the name of Jesus!! Woman of God, I cover you, in Jesus' name. Amen.

ABOUT THE AUTHOR

Maja Hodo was born and raised in Georgia, where she and her husband of ten years are raising three beautiful children.

She is a first-time author and hopes to inspire many by continuing to write life-transforming books to help women of all ages.

It's her mission to encourage, empower, and enlighten women as she keeps sharing the Gospel with a hint of her life story and testimony.

Social Media
Facebook: Maja Hodo
Instagram: women_of_worth_orm
Website: womenofworthorm.com

CHAPTER 4

The Warrior Awakens: Brokenness, My Northern Star

by Amanda Cohodes

Iwoke up in the hotel room that morning with my baby girl, and I knew it was about to be the best day of my life. It was a quiet and cool fall day. You could hear a gentle breeze rustling through the trees. That morning, he had left a box on the table with a note, "For the gift God gave me. See you at the church." Yes, it was my wedding day. The day I dreamt about since I was little, was finally here. Finally, I was going to have the family I'd longed for my whole life. I didn't have a care in the world that day; I was marrying my best friend.

I wasn't the only one who was excited. My daughter Kaitlyn couldn't wait to put on her dress. She looked like a princess in a white gown with purple flower accents throughout the bottom of the dress. Purple is our favorite color, and the day wouldn't be right without it. Kaitlyn had no idea that she was the one who prepared me for this day. She was the northern star that brought me to my knees and made me cry out for Jesus to come into my life. I considered the risks of marriage, and I was dead set against divorce ever being an option. I looked forward to building an empire and taking the devil out with the most solid union. My wedding day was the calm before the storm that would leave me shipwrecked, in despair, and lost in a wilderness that I thought I might never escape.

The biggest endeavor I ever undertook was planning a wedding. I was so blessed that my friends from my small group bible study had accompanied me to create my vision for that day. From decorating the hall to the sanctuary to the flower arrangements and the table centerpieces, they stood beside me throughout every detail. My dear friend Michele would also stand beside me as a bridesmaid. They all just wanted to show me, such agape love.

I never believed I was worthy of being a wife. Growing up Jewish, after 30, well, they just count you out. So, to be 33 years old and a bride, I was so excited! In the Jewish faith and culture, so much emphasis is placed on marriage, and your completion in faith comes with building a home with your husband. Every Jewish girl learns how to have a family, and she knows her way around the kitchen. Judaism has very traditional gender roles. I wanted to make sure to have everything just right because it was supposed to be the happiest day of my life.

I can still say to this day that my wedding day is a memory I cherish. You may ask, "Why is she saying this?" After a divorce and the mess that ensued, her wedding is still her favorite day? I know it seems crazy, but when I looked in the mirror that day, I had not one negative thing to say about myself. I looked beautiful, and I felt like a Queen. In that oyster-colored wedding dress, I saw the Woman of God He created. I saw myself as Jesus saw me—perfect in His eyes. I thought I couldn't wear a white dress because I'd had a child out of wedlock which meant there was nothing pure about me. The oyster color looked better, and it allowed me to hold onto the idea that I was unworthy to wear white.

Throughout my life, I had high standards and was disappointed by the consequences of my choices. Let me assure you that I do not regret getting pregnant at 24, although I wasn't married. I knew my wedding day would be my redemption story. Everything came together; Kaitlyn loved him, and her dad got along with my future husband very well. All these things ran through my mind as I got ready for my big day.

I was all smiles as we gathered in the community room of the church when it was time to get ready. I will never forget the moment when Kaitlyn hugged me and leaned her head into my side as I stood there in my wedding dress. She said, "Mama, you look beautiful, and I love you." That blonde-haired, blue-eyed girl was my angel. God knew I needed her more than she needed me. If I was going to walk down that aisle, it was because we were all going to be happy.

I walked towards the sanctuary, where I saw my groom waiting at the front of the church. We decided to take pictures before the service and wanted our first photos to be private, as the tension between our families was challenging and stressful to our relationship. He stood there crying as we embraced. It was a magical moment.

This special day was all about the details. I remember the piano playing and walking down the aisle, and I kept looking forward because 190 people were in that church to celebrate us. Although the man I married loved to be in the limelight, I am more reserved. To stand in the center of the sanctuary and have everyone's eyes on me made me nervous, not to mention I was about to bear my heart to this man through my vows. I was shaking on the inside as I walked down the aisle with my dad. I could feel Dad's anxiety as we approached the altar. I had never seen him emotional until the moment he placed my hands into my husband's. My dad whispered, "Take care of my baby." As he turned to the stairs, I saw his eyes fill with tears, and he tripped on the way down the stairs.

That is another reason I loved my wedding day. My dad is an amazing guy, but he had such a tough time expressing himself. However, on my wedding day, I realized how much he loved me. I am grateful for that moment because it was my dad who became my biggest rock, next to God, in the storm that raged in the weeks and months ahead.

We performed the ceremony, exchanging our vows and personal statements, followed by the sand ceremony that symbolized the two of us becoming one. Before we got to the sand ceremony, one of the most special moments occurred. Remember when I mentioned earlier, the box left on the table? In it, was a rose gold, custom diamond cross. My husband knew I wasn't one for jewelry, but this was something I would wear always. He also bought a cross for Kaitlyn, and when he put it on her neck, I got emotional. He told her, she wasn't biologically his, but God had given her to him, and he would always be there for her. At the time, I thought that was the most beautiful moment, but it ended up being the hardest moment to forgive him for in the end.

When the wedding ceremony ended, my husband crushed a glass with his foot—a Jewish tradition symbolizing the crushing of the old life and the beginning of a new one as husband and wife.

As we headed to our reception, I was at such peace. Everything flowed so smoothly. As a child, I grew up in chaos, so to have a day without strife or challenges was such a relief. It is amazing to me that when you are going through something, you miss the signals that God places in your path. Looking back at the reception, I remember dancing most of the night with Kaitlyn on the dance floor. My husband was worried about entertaining our guests and rarely spent time with me that night. We ate next to each other, shared a few dances, and I never realized how he valued who I was is in his life as his actions did not match his words.

We already had challenges before we got married. We were in couples' therapy for a long time as we had difficulty with communication because we handled conflict differently. This is something that became very apparent on our honeymoon, as we fought almost every night we were in Mexico. I recall looking on my phone to see about changing my flight to go home early. I was living in a fantasy and wanted to believe the situation I was in was better than it was. I was slowly losing who I was. Day by day, Amanda was being erased.

I grew up in a very abusive, dysfunctional household, and I navigated abuse well. It was the second language I was fluent in. So often, we would rather be with someone than be alone, and even if that person isn't good for us, it beats the feeling of loneliness. The night before I married him, my ex-husband asked me what my biggest fear was. I shared with him that it was to end up on the third floor of the McHenry County courthouse in divorce court. It wasn't that I was afraid of a divorce, it was the memory of years of fighting for my daughter in a custody battle that scared me.

I went through a challenging process to become the woman I became in marriage. The difficulties started on December 23, 2010. I was on my way home from work, and at the time, I was an electronics sales associate at Wal-Mart. I was excited to see my almost 18-month-old daughter. Then my world flipped upside down, and I would never be the same.

I was greeted in my driveway by five squad cars. Police approached me as I got out of my car to walk towards the house. "Amanda, stop where you are!" I heard them yell. Of course, I stopped, they had served me with an Order of Protection. I had no idea what was going on. All I knew was that I had my car and the clothes on my back, and I had to leave the property. I was confused and afraid. I couldn't even get my medications. It was so scary because I didn't know what I did wrong, and I wouldn't find out until my court date.

I got into my Accord and drove off, parked in a parking lot, and cried my eyes out. I yelled at God, "Where are you and how is this happening?!" I read the legal papers and understood I could have no direct or third-party contact. That is just a fancy way of saying I couldn't contact my family or my daughter through a mutual party. I couldn't even send her a Christmas gift.

I was terrified of what might happen. I took my phone out and called my brother, aunts, uncles, and cousins as I wanted to know if I could stay with someone. Everyone said no. I wasn't surprised, as, in a narcissistic family, you must have a backbone to resist.

Next, I began to call friends. One friend—I will call her T—welcomed me to her home. I spent a few days at her house until I found an apartment. That was a Godsend. I didn't know Jesus then, but T was the definition of a woman who loved Jesus and people. She was a friend in the worst of times, and our conversations during those few nights softened my heart and transformed it.

I went out on T's back porch on Christmas morning and yelled at the top of my lungs, "Merry Christmas, Toubie!" Toubie was my nickname for Kaitlyn since birth. I hadn't bonded tightly with my daughter because I didn't know how. In this situation, I didn't know or see where God was, but His hand of favor was on my life. This event would lead me to Christ and free me from the toxic family system I grew up in. I just didn't know it then.

The following week I met with a lawyer and contacted a domestic violence agency that the police suggested I call after the holidays. The lawyer put in requests to get copies of the full filing (order of protection) and I looked for an apartment. I couldn't stay at friends' houses forever; I was too independent for that. I quickly found a one-bedroom apartment and settled into a new life, as I counted the days until I would go to court.

When the day finally came, I was mortified by the false allegations filed by my mother and Kaitlyn's father with the Department of Children and Family Services. They were absurd, but that day my heart shattered when the judge put my daughter in the temporary custody of my mother, as Kaitlyn's father lived with them. It would be several more weeks until I got to see my baby girl. It was so much to bear, and I didn't know how I was going to, so I prayed.

An advocate from the domestic violence agency started coming to court to help me regain custody of my baby. Eventually, a few weeks before Kaitlyn's 2nd birthday on February 19th, I was granted supervised visitation. I paid $280 a week to see my daughter, and I wasn't even guilty of the allegations—it was the judicial process. I was so excited to see her but never had to control my emotions more than on that day. I bought her tons of balloons, presents, and of course, a cake. That visit was especially emotional because it wasn't looking good for me in court.

I decided to have Kaitlyn baptized. I knew she belonged to God before she was given to me, so into his hands, I committed her. The advocate belonged to the same church, so we planned the event. That morning as I walked into the church with my heart beating so fast, I had to have the faith of Abraham to trust that even though my court situation didn't look good, God had always been faithful, and I knew He would be faithful again.

Months later, I received partial custody of Kaitlyn, and she came to stay with me at my apartment. My heart couldn't have been happier, but I was still undergoing a process. My entire family were witnesses for my ex, Kaitlyn's dad, and that hurt deeply.

Before the trial, I got a tattoo on my inner calf of a cross with 1st Corinthians 13 summarized in it. The cross is all black because this life will bring you trouble, and it's not always easy in this world. The butterflies represent the beauty of meeting Jesus—pink for Kaitlyn—and blue, a prophetic revelation about Samuel Isaiah, a son I later lost in miscarriage. I walked into the court for the trial wearing a suit, with my head held high. I touched my pant leg, where underneath, the cross tattoo reminded me that God was with me as I sat through the nightmare.

On October 1, 2011, my custody situation still wasn't resolved, but I decided to get baptized on my birthday. I was going all in for Jesus, and I wanted the world to know that despite the trial, I had hope for God's provision. I trusted His ways more than my own. So often, we want to end our pain, but it is through struggle that we grow. That day, I transitioned into my new skin.

A part of me felt like I was betraying my family. My parents had spent so much money and time on my religious education. I was the girl who blew the shofar on high holidays and was studying to become a rabbi. How would I publicly declare I was following Jesus? I wrestled with my thoughts and realized for the first time that I was deciding for myself, and what others thought about it wasn't important. That was truly a first for me. I was used to being what everyone wanted me to be, a people-pleaser. This time, it was about destiny, and God knew that if He didn't separate me from my family, my heart would never be open to discovering who I was meant to be.

I know I am different. I have this gift of love. It is easier for me to love than hold onto negative emotions. At the time, it was easier for me to let everyone but me off the hook because of my perfectionism. The custody situation broke my heart in ways I never knew were possible. However, to be made whole, we must first accept that we are broken. I have found that in that brokenness, our vulnerability surfaces, but God can restore us. This restoration process takes time, and it happens on various levels. What this experience and divorce taught me, is that until faulty systems are destroyed, a new foundation can never be laid. One cannot build a new life on a cracked foundation. We must first repair those cracks and then rebuild, stronger. God was healing me, but first, I had to be cracked open and pressed like an olive.

It may seem weird, but my baptism was one of my best birthdays ever. It was something that I chose; I was the priority. That was a first for me. In fact, I just realized it while writing this chapter. I never chose myself. I created myself as other. One of the biggest mistakes I ever made was not seeing my gifts and believing I was less than. Baptism was the connection I had to my baby girl. I was prepared to lose her, knowing we would always be connected in faith. This was the beginning of witnessing my first miracle.

Looking back, I see God's fingerprints on my life through this custody battle and divorce. He was developing the warrior inside of me. I never knew it, but she was in there, locked away, roaring. We all have a voice, and my voice had been silenced a long time ago.

I had an awakening recently, in August 2021, in South Africa. I found Mandy (the younger me) there, and I began to fall in love with her, all of her, the good and the bad. If I had any advice for the younger me, it would be, don't wait to love who you are. Run after your dreams even if everyone doubts you and laughs.

I never understood that becoming a mother, a job I never wanted, was exactly what I was called to. I was created to break the chains of generational curses. Kaitlyn is the missing piece that keeps me focused on the bigger picture. Quitting was not an option, so I learned how to fight—knee mail.

I prayed for hours, and on my days off, I sat with my bible under a tree and meditated on scripture. I always had a thirst for meeting God. That is another gift God gave me—I am authentic. God knows how I feel, and I never stop investing in our relationship. I talk to God like he is sitting right next to me, like a friend. I believe that is one of the reasons I have seen God at work in my life so much. I need God every moment. I know God heard the cry of my heart every night that I fell asleep alone. He filled my heart with the wisdom to make good choices during that time. I took all sorts of parenting classes, attended counseling, and started healing my traumas. I knew that I had no idea how to raise a healthy child, but I was determined to learn all I could. As I went through this process, I realized my inner child was hurting badly, and I needed time to heal. This time away from Kaitlyn hurt, but it was necessary to prepare me for my call.

I remember the morning of September 18, 2012. It was the day I saw my first miracle. I prepared for the court that morning with loud praise music, my suit steamed and pressed, shoes polished, and I applied makeup. I would wake up at around 3:00 a.m. on the mornings I had a court appointment. In the first hour, I read scripture. During the second hour, I prayed aloud, and then I made breakfast and went about my routine. On the way to court, I would always play the same song: "Brave" by Nicole Nordeman. I love a line in that song, "So long... status quo, I think I just let go, you make me wanna be brave." God made me want to be brave. It was not on my strength but in His that I could hold my head high.

When I walked into the courtroom that morning, my palms were sweaty, my heart pounded, and my mind was a cloud of confusion. Still a baby Christian, I was learning how to trust God. I wanted some level of control, but I had none. It was in all the days prior that I realized God's hands were truly on me. I thought I was going to lose custody, but the court granted me sole custody. That was a better outcome than I had ever dreamed. I hoped for joint residential custody, but God knew what Kaitlyn needed, and He showed up! So now, when things look difficult, I pray because I remind myself that God has always been faithful even if things don't look how I want them to.

I share this part of my story because God should always have credibility with us, but sometimes seeing victories in situations helps to build our faith. It was because I saw God provide for me in the custody battle that I could trust Him to hold my hand as I navigated the storm of divorce. God wants to be number one in our lives, and when we go wayward, He does not spare us from the pain of following our will. He never promises it will be easy; He promises that He will be with us.

I lived in fantasy because I had not yet fully fallen in love with myself. That is one of the beautiful gifts I was given by my ex-husband—he taught me I am beautiful.

When divorce occurs, it doesn't mean either party is wrong, it means you're not walking the same path. I remember standing in front of a mountain in Sandy, Utah, realizing that my husband and I were no longer aligned. After months of praying for reconciliation, it was on that business trip with a company called Yoli, that I realized I had to file for divorce. I couldn't wait anymore. It was the most difficult decision I ever made. All I wanted my whole life was to be married and have a family, and I failed. I chose wrong. What made it more difficult was that I never got closure. I just got a text message: "Amanda, I want a divorce." I felt that if he wanted a divorce, he should have filed for it, but I would have been waiting forever.

When he first left, Kaitlyn said, "Mommy, delete him." I have to say, my daughter was wise beyond her years. I remember the pain of being shattered. I didn't know my worth at the time. Ladies, until you know who you are and the value you offer, don't entertain marriage. It is the most important decision you will ever make. That is one thing I would tell myself if I could go back. I listened to my ex-husband's words, but his actions never followed. I realize now that he married me because he knew I wanted marriage. In that marriage, I lost who I was.

The biggest sin I ever committed was putting someone before my relationship with God. I was so obsessed with trying to keep my husband happy that I forgot about myself. Divorce has taught me to guard my heart and always invest in my relationship with God. If you take your eyes off Jesus even for a moment, like Peter, you could start to sink into the water.

This decision to marry the wrong person destroyed me. That Amanda was destroyed. It was the most painful experience of my life other than losing Kaitlyn. I sacrificed myself for breadcrumbs of love and that is not what God intended marriage to be. What did I expect? I was a broken woman. A broken woman and a broken man can never have a healthy marriage. Marriage is about two whole individuals creating a life together. Our relationship was falsely perfect, and perfect doesn't last. I won't go into details, but in that relationship, I experienced a lot of abuse: physical, emotional, financial, and even spiritual. I share this because if you're in a toxic relationship, I want you to know there is hope and healing afterwards. It is challenging work, but if you are willing to do the work, life on the other side is more beautiful than you can imagine.

I recall the car ride to the courthouse to file the paperwork. My friend Michele, who stood by me as I made my marriage vows, was there to walk beside me as I faced my biggest fear, the third-floor divorce court. My hands trembled as I opened the doors to the Clerk's office. Michele was so patient with me as I cried and filled out the paperwork. Nothing is harder to do than something that is not the desire of your heart. I have never been more grateful for a godly friend to sit beside me in my darkest hour. It took several weeks for the court to serve my husband with the divorce papers, and then we started the proceedings, which took several months. When everything between us was agreed upon, they scheduled the court date.

I walked into that courtroom on December 17th and held my composure, praise be to God. When the judge granted the divorce, I realized I was free, but not whole. I was a bird in a cage with broken wings, but the cage door was open. God could now get to work in my heart to heal me.

For the longest time, I was angry at God. What I value the most is love, and I gave God my marriage. I valued the vow I made on my wedding day, and I felt like such a failure walking out of the courtroom. It was not until six months after that I fully realized how God provisioned for me.

It was during a day at counseling. Kaitlyn has autism, and it is a part of our routine to help her overcome challenges. She spoke to the counselor about how happy she was that my ex-husband was gone. She said it made her sad he didn't say goodbye, but she didn't like seeing mommy hit and yelled at. We often never realize that our children are watching us, and the divorce sent a message to her that I was valuable. My daughter has taught me so much about life through her different lens.

My divorce broke the cycle of abuse in my family. It was the beginning of a bigger plan of healing and testimony. Mom and Dad are both still Jewish, but through my divorce, they saw a strength that could only be a testimony of God's hand in my life. My relationship with my dad was healed in many ways. The most impactful moment was when he shared how painful it was for him to see another man hit me because he taught me it was OK. His apology meant the world to me. What I have come to realize is that there is no manual to being the perfect parent, but there is a way to validate, illustrate, and teach a child. When we make mistakes, we take ownership and apologize.

Sometimes life can be hard. Sometimes we don't understand in our humanness what God is doing. His plans are perfect. If I had never lost my daughter, I would have never found my faith in Christ. If I had no faith in Christ, I would never have survived the divorce, or the healing needed to birth my calling. Sometimes we go through trials for people we meet along our journey. What hurt so bad at one point, has helped encourage so many people I have encountered.

Abuse used to define me, but I have developed an inner strength I never thought I had. When my heart broke in divorce, it allowed me to fall in love with myself. I know who I am, and I am so proud of the woman I met on my wedding day. She is a world changer. She is strong and courageous, and she is beautiful. My pastor at the time, Lisa Kruse-Safford, shared something with me that became my mantra in divorce. I am strong, able, and healed. That is exactly what God has been faithful to. He continues to redeem and restore the woman He created me to be. Sometimes we must weather the darkness to realize the light that dwells within. I am so grateful that God never stopped pursuing me. My heart belongs to Him. If I can teach Kaitlyn anything, it is always to trust God. No one has ever loved me like my Abba (Hebrew name for God).

ABOUT THE AUTHOR

Amanda Cohodes holds a Bachelor of Science degree in Business Administration & Accounting from DeVry University. She is a member of the Sigma Beta Delta National Honors Society. Amanda is the owner of Amanda Cohodes Accounting & Tax and Triune Dream Builders, a Licensed Insurance Professional, and a Certified Professional Life Coach with a concentration in Empowerment, Domestic Violence and Mindset.

Amanda currently serves three non-profit agencies, Church Beyond the Walls, Coaching Forward International, and Complete Women Ministries. Amanda is a local and global missionary working with the homeless, orphans, and disadvantaged communities. She has recently traveled to South Africa and continues to be involved in planning and financial support for missions in Costa Rica and South Africa.

Amanda previously served on the Board of Directors of the McHenry County chapter of NAMI (National Alliance on Mental Illness). She also served as the Community Representative & Assistant Treasurer for Northern Illinois Emmaus and was the Financial Administrator/Community Advocate of Foundations for Living/Peace4All Domestic Violence Agency. Her passion is education and empowerment. She enjoys teaching financial literacy and entrepreneurship to diverse populations.

Amanda is the proud mother of Kaitlyn, who lives with autism. In her free time, she spends time with her daughter, two dogs, Triston and Layla, or in the gym pursuing her passion for bodybuilding.

In the future, Amanda Cohodes plans to continue to travel globally. She hopes to lead mission teams to empower, teach entrepreneurial skills to locals, and build stronger communities globally.

CHAPTER 5

Unspoken Truth

by Quana Leon

Have you ever been at a place in your life when you asked yourself how did I get caught up in this situation? I have, repeatedly. Allow me to elaborate.

It was a hot summer day when out came this ten-pound, nine-ounce baby girl named Quana. I was my mother's 40th birthday gift. It was the night of Mom's birthday when my father, who she had not seen in almost twenty years, suddenly showed up and scooped her up for a night out to celebrate. Despite their rocky past, which included him hitting her and having a wife that he had not told her about, she thought he was the love of her life. She was so excited to see him that night! I arrived in the world exactly nine months later.

When the nurse saw my dad, she said, yup, she's yours. He could not deny that I belonged to his bloodline, but that did not make us family. My dad had several sets of children from his multiple women, and they still refuse to have a relationship with me except for my two brothers. One brother died years ago, and the other helps fill in the blanks of my many questions. As a woman, I can only imagine how hard a decision it was to bring a baby into the world by a man who already had a family. I don't know if I could have done it, knowing that she would be fatherless.

Memories of My Father

I knew that my father existed and who he was, but he was not a factor in my life. When I think about my father, not many memories come to mind. I remember him being tall and very handsome. He had a perfect smile with deep dimples and one gold tooth on the side. He was well-dressed and wore a black leather jacket like Shaft. I can still hear his footsteps; they always sounded like he was wearing heels. I even remember him being at my preschool graduation. He was not around much, and if he was, he was more concerned with seeing my mother, not me.

I was 11 years old the last time I saw my father. He was in the hospital. I visited him, he hugged me, and I kissed him on his cheek. He asked about school and how I was getting so big. I hadn't seen him in years. When I went back to the hospital about a month later, I walked by him. I did not even recognize him. I asked my mother, where is he? I couldn't understand, at that young age, what had happened to him. My father was dying. When I walked over to him and stared at his sunken eyes, he began to cry. Tears fell in buckets down his face. His stomach, legs, and hands were swollen. I wondered if he was crying because he regretted realizing he could not make up the time we lost. I will never know.

From the Projects to South Carolina

I lived in New York City projects. When the streetlights came on, I had to go into the house. Living in the projects was like being surrounded by a big family. As the youngest child in the family, all eyes were on me. Everybody knew everybody, and if I were out of order, my neighborhood moms would get me right—and my mother permitted them. Everything you can imagine happened on my block. There were drug dealers, their runners, crackheads, fiends, prostitutes, and abusers around, all the time. There was an unspoken truth in the projects that was never up for discussion.

I was known for fighting because my older sister was a beast. When someone disrespected me verbally, pushed me, or threatened to do something to me, she made me fight them and dared anybody to jump in. They knew she was nothing to play with. Even if I didn't want to fight, she would say her famous words, "If you don't whip them, I'm goin' whip you myself," so I had to give them the business and fight them. Although I was a fighter when I was younger, I couldn't fight my way out of domestic violence.

In 1997, in my junior year of high school, my mother decided to relocate us to South Carolina. I was so angry with her. I was in the prime of my teenage years.

I managed a dance group of little girls and created our music mix and choreography. They performed at the Apollo Theater and many other venues in the tri-state area, this was opening so many doors for me, and at that time you couldn't tell me we were not going to be something big. My best friend and I attempted to run away, but that plan failed quickly because our money was low. I wanted to stay with my sister and finish school in the city. All the planning I did to graduate with my friends went out the window. My mother had a habit of making decisions based on her best interests, not mine. I wish she would have at least asked me or allowed me to voice my opinion on how that move might affect me.

Throughout my last year of high school, when my classmates were going to games on Friday night or to parties, I couldn't go. I was not allowed to sleep over either. I was always at home, babysitting. Mom didn't mind if I had company, whether she was home or not, but leaving the house was not an option.

In the summer of 1998—we lived in South Carolina for about a year —my friend took me to a football game where I met Tony. He was very attractive and bowlegged. We didn't hit it off right away because he had that thick country accent, and I was used to those slick-talking city boys. Tony was very outgoing. He could come and go to his mom's house as he pleased, but my mother wasn't playing that. It took me a long time to see his true colors.

In 1999 on my 18th birthday, I moved out. It was my first taste of freedom. I could come and go as I wanted to, and I didn't have to babysit kids or look after anyone. I learned the responsibility of being on my own during the first month when those bills came in.

I was still dating my high school boyfriend. Living on my own, I could spend time with him whenever I felt like it. He wanted to live with me, but I wasn't anybody's fool. I had just got my independence, and I was not about to give it up for a boyfriend who was just like me, fresh out of high school and unsure of his plans.

Tony still lived with his mom, and he was so much fun at my place, but at home, he was different. People kept knocking on the door for him, and he was in and out. Sometimes he would stare off and not say much. I didn't understand why there was such a change in his personality. I would go into the kitchen to ask his mom what was wrong with him, and mid-way through my conversation, she would lean over as if falling asleep. Before she hit the floor, she'd jump back up and ask me what I said. She knew but never would tell me anything. Later, I found out that Tony was doing cocaine and his mother was on heroin, but then, I was clueless.

On New Year's Eve night 2000, my mom had a small gathering. A couple of friends and I decided to meet at Mom's for some drinks before we headed to the club. On our way to the club, I felt sick. When we arrived at the club parking lot, I threw up, and it was so bad, I couldn't go in. I told them to leave me in the car and to enjoy themselves. When I got home, my apartment doors were kicked in, and the R&B music I left on was still playing. I looked to see if anything was missing, and nothing was. I called around to let Tony know, and low and behold, it was him. He claimed he thought I was in there cheating because he heard some slow jams playing. I was pissed off, thinking, how dare you break into my place!

God's Got Another Plan

A few weeks later, my sister came into town to visit me, and I told her that I had a stomach virus and a cold. She interrupted me and said, "You are pregnant." I was like, "Girl, you are bugging!" She began pressing on my breasts, telling me they looked larger. We went back and forth about why I was feeling that way. Finally, she convinced me to go to the ER. They asked me about my last menstrual cycle. I didn't remember. I'd lost track of timing, so the nurse gave me a urine test. Thirty minutes passed when the doctor came in wearing a stupid grin. Congratulations, you are pregnant.

I waited seven days before I told Tony because I was confused about my feelings and who I wanted to know. It happened so fast, and I could not believe it. I was so mad at myself that I didn't know what to do or how to feel. I was ashamed and embarrassed at the same time. He was so excited, and so were our families. I was about to be someone's mom, and I didn't think I wanted to. I did not want to be responsible for another person again. It was too late as I was six weeks pregnant.

I was almost three months pregnant when I started to forgive myself as I mentally prepared for my child. We left for our doctor's appointment and were happily planning on moving in together to raise our baby. However, God had another plan. The doctor told us that they couldn't find the heartbeat and that I had miscarried. I couldn't catch my breath. I sobbed uncontrollably. My boyfriend yelled at the doctor, asking how this happened, what went wrong, and if we could try again. Tony turned to me and asked, "What did you do?" The doctor said the baby's heartbeat had stopped, and it should pass within a few days. Those days felt like months. I didn't understand why they thought it was psychologically OK to leave the dead baby inside my body until it passed. I had to remind myself to breathe and that this was part of the process.

Thinking about what Tony asked me at the doctor's bothered me. A month later, the doctor performed a DNC with my mother by my side. Tony was in jail.

As it was, with every other death, people called and visited, but then that ended. I felt alone and as if I was the only woman on earth that had experienced this type of pain. Being alone, I could think about what I wanted and the people I surrounded myself with. Having my independence was fun, but I realized I was also irresponsible and I didn't want to be with Tony anymore. I broke up with my boyfriend by sending him a letter in jail. He wrote back telling me he understood, and we could talk further when he got out in 90 days. I began to read self-help books to build up my strength so that I wouldn't look back.

In 2001 I went to my friend's Mimi cookout and met Red. He was nonchalant. He was also from another city, so I knew he didn't know Tony or his people. We bonded instantly. He would come over to my house and help me clean for my mom. He kept my car clean and the gas tank full. He was the guy friend I needed at the time. When I took him to the burnside of town, he high-fived people that knew Tony. I started to wonder how he knew them. He would say from the club or another person he knew, but he never mentioned he was Tony's cousin. With that news, I knew it was over.

A Hard Lesson in Trust

September 2001; it was a Sunday I have never forgotten. My mom was at church, and I met a friend at her house. I left her screen door open. The house was in the country, and you had to be going to see someone there because you would not be just passing by. The doorbell rang as I had just got dressed to head out. I was wearing a blue jean dress with brown trimming and these cute brown clogs to match. When I got to the door, I saw Tony. I was shocked because I didn't know he was out of jail. "What are you doing here?" I asked. That fool said, "I'm coming to get you." I laughed because the guy Tony was with was his cousin Red, so I asked him, "What is Tony is talking about?" He didn't say anything. They picked me up and put me in the back seat of the car. The doors were on childproof lock so I couldn't get out. I fought for my life, kicking, punching, and scratching Tony. The man struggled to hold me down because his nose was bleeding from one of my many kicks. He was high on cocaine and felt nothing. Tony was hallucinating that I wanted him back after all that time. I knew it had to be God stepping in because that back window opened, and I unlocked the door. I ran out screaming and yelling, with only my panties on because Tony had snatched my dress off.

They chased me and put me back in the car. Tony looked for something to tie my hands and feet with because I kept kicking the car out of gear. I talked to Red while I was crying, asking him, "What you are doing and why are you letting him force you?" I saw the fear on his face too. It was like we were both trapped. For some unknown reason, they decided to return to Mom's house. They didn't have the decency to drive me into the yard but let me out on the street and skidded off. I ran into the house, screaming. My mother yelled, "Quana, what's wrong? Talk to me!" I cried hysterically, naked. Zeus, my brother, grabbed a blanket for me. Somebody called the cops. The sheriff showed up. While the forensic team took pictures of my body, Red called to apologize. The cops asked me to keep him on the phone so that they could catch them, and they did just that. Small-town news travels very fast. The police wrote out a report and immediately put in a request for an order of protection. I couldn't help but wonder what the hell they wanted to do with me and how it could have ended worse than that. I thank God for my praying mother because her faith and relationship with Jesus covered me.

Regardless of the excitement of living on my own, that ended because of the trauma I experienced. I was depressed and sleep didn't come easy in my apartment. I was always jumpy and paranoid. I called my mom and asked if could move back home, and I did. I started spending more time with my sister and traveled to get my mind off the pain and the fact that I was so naïve. I learned the hard way that drug use can cause a person to have more than one personality. You never know who is going to show up.

A New Man, A New Pain

In 2003 When I met Calvin, I was honest and explained to him that I wasn't ready for a relationship. He patiently waited for me with no pressure as he was very easy-going. This man was smart, noticeably confident, and not of the streets, or so, I thought. He worked for a good company and was a good provider. I decided to live with him, and I wanted for nothing in the beginning. We talked about traveling and wanted to have a family. I was already in love with his son so, I could see this happening. My family thought he was it and were over the moon.

I learned that people switch their behavior with you when they feel you are isolated from your family and friends. When I pillow-talked, I told him about doing so many things for others, and he said things like, "Your mom doesn't appreciate you for helping her out. You always running for your family, but when are they going to start doing for you?"

Case in point, shortly after we started dating, but before I had the opportunity to move in with him, I left to go to New York to help my sister with her children while she got acclimated to her new job. My intention was not to stay long, but due to 9/11, my trip got extended.

He was right to a certain point, or at least this is what I thought but didn't say out loud. I returned from New York six months later and moved in with him. That is when he changed. He no longer liked what I was wearing and bought me an entirely new wardrobe. I found myself visiting friends and family less, and whenever any of my girls came to see me, he insinuated they were always flirting with him. He became more controlling and isolating as time went on.

Two years into the relationship, I was standing in front of my house talking to one of his friends who had been looking for him, and this man pulled up, screeching tires. He got out of the car so fast, pushed me in the door, and slapped me. I was in shock. I couldn't even speak. As I headed to the front door of the apartment, he suddenly kicked me in the back. He tried to push me over the balcony, saying I disrespected him by talking with a man in front of his house. This made no sense to me because this was Calvin's friend knocking on the door looking for him. He felt comfortable doing this because I was totally dependent on him, and he knew it. I tried to hide the bruises that were on my body. He was smart enough not to bruise my face.

I left him and went back to my mother's house. However, it was crowded, with my brother and his girlfriend, my niece and nephew living there, my nephew, who wore the same size shoes as me, would steal my sneakers. Because of the lack of privacy, I went back to live with Calvin.

He said he was sorry and it wouldn't happen again, but that was a lie. I suffered in silence for another year and a half because I was embarrassed, and the one thing I said I wouldn't accept from a man was right in my face. He didn't put his hands on me for a while, and I thought he had changed.

However, one day as I talked to the guys from my block, he overheard them telling me how things had changed, and we were all grown up now. I'm not going to lie; they were a bit graphic with details, but these were my friends, and there was no need to be jealous. He came into the room, grabbed me by the ponytail, and pulled me up the hall. We started fighting, and I called the police. He ran somewhere, and they couldn't find him.

I didn't have a license, but I had a car registered in both our names and a gun in my hand. An officer from Jersey warned me and told me to drive to my mother's house and that if I got stopped, to give them the yellow paper. The next day, Calvin came out and took the car back. I should have told my family what was going on. I just couldn't find the nerve. He was a broken man a long time before I met him. I just didn't see it, because, like a sheep in wolf's clothing, he hid his true self from me.

The reason I stayed was that I was young and very materialistic. I led myself to believe he would get better with time. I made excuses for his behavior. The catalyst that led me to leave was when this man pulled me out of my apartment, and I screamed, asking people to help, and no one did. I could see them in their windows, and they did nothing. I managed to get away and was heading to my car, and as he was about to throw a dorm trunk at me, I blacked out, shot at him, and left.

The police went to my mother's house looking for me, and when I called her, she was crying, asking me what I had done and why the police were there looking for me. At this point, I thought I had killed him. All I could do was think if I had left when the violence first started or spoken up about it, it wouldn't have gone this far. I almost gave up my future. But as I looked at the present, I turned myself in.

When I arrived at the precinct, I found out he was alive and well. I had missed. The judge took my license to carry a weapon away and marked the offense of domestic violence on my criminal record. When I got out of jail, the detective gave me the DV number to seek help if this happened again.

Even after that, he stalked me and broke into my house. It was not easy to get away or leave, but I did.

Finding My Way Out of Darkness

When I left Calvin, I thought that was the end of that chapter in my life. Going through that turmoil changed the way I handled men. I left the physical abuse behind, but the mental abuse framed the decisions I made going forward. I constantly asked myself if I was good enough, smart enough, pretty enough. I blamed all those uncomfortable feelings on him and what he did to me, but honestly, the blame was mutual. I could not control what he did, but I allowed it.

I had no respect for men, and intimacy was far from my mind. For my sanity and growth, I focused on myself and my needs. I got a great job and was very successful at the company I worked for. I met some real-life friends along the way. I was in a great place until a promotion required me to have a degree. That's when my past hit me in the face. With the domestic violence charge on my record, that promotion was denied. I had left that man, but he found a way to haunt me.

I went through the steps to try to remove that charge from my criminal record. I filed for an appeal, but the judge denied it. I didn't meet the requirement for an expungement. I wanted to study law in college but would not be able to sit for the bar. So, I chose to pursue a degree in business.

While attaining my degree, I found my passion and started a virtual assistance company, AOEVA. I was very successful and had clients across the country. It was a source of pride to create something that allowed me to do what I loved and was good at. It was not easy while juggling school, work, and life, but I did it. I graduated from college. My supporters came out, in numbers, to celebrate me, and I felt so blessed.

It had been fifteen years when I decided to file for a pardon. I had to have three references and a career history. I had to write to the courts explaining why I deserved to have my rights restored. It was a long journey to get back to the person I was before I allowed that man to ruin my life. Thank God I accomplished that and regained my rights as a citizen.

When a person controls your mind, they don't have to worry about your actions. When a person manipulates you into believing they know what's best for you, you lose your power. You start to fear your judgment, and your actions are led by them. Domestic violence doesn't happen overnight. It happens slowly and methodically. I was like his prey. He studied me, learned my weaknesses, and used them against me. He became everything I was looking for until the mask fell off. I wish I had followed the signs. I was young, and that isn't an excuse, but I didn't use the women's intuition that God gave me. I was unaware of my power. Everything I was looking for from him was, in fact, within me.

I had to learn not to be so hard on myself and praise my little wins like leaving, staying away, and believing in myself. Family and friends are very important. I was afraid to be transparent with my family because I thought I stayed away too long. However, they were waiting on me with open arms. My family kept an eye on me or a voice in my ear. I no longer feel alone.

ABOUT THE AUTHOR

 Quana Leon is the Founder and CEO of Array of Essence non-profit organization that assists individuals with establishing their place in society. It provides its clients with safe housing, career coaching, where to find affordable clothing for interviews, and other community resources based on their unique needs.

Developing relationships with her clients led Quana to pursue her certification as an accountability and relationship coach. Quana empowers her clients to explore what is possible and coaches them to accomplish it. She holds a Degree in Health Information Management which allowed her to be financially responsible while pursuing her goals. Quana is a woman of God, wife, and mother.

CHAPTER 6

Pretty Rejected

by Robyn L. Rease

Mamie walked assuredly down the long hallway of the shot-gun house she purchased for a few hundred dollars she saved from her work as a domestic for the Leeves of Warrington, Florida. The bright white house was trimmed in black and had a welcoming front porch painted brick red. From the kitchen in the very back of the house to the front door was a straight shot, which coined the term for this style of home. Mamie moved like Harriet Tubman from the kitchen towards the door as if a slave needed her to set them free. In her mind, that was indeed the mission. The slave was my mother, Brenda, and the slave-master was my father, Lawrence, who was approaching the chain-link fence to pick me up to take me for a ride. He had come home to Pensacola from Jacksonville where he was stationed in the

US Navy. He had two destinations in Pensacola: his childhood home on Indigo Street where his mom and some of his siblings still lived, and the shotgun house on Beach Street where I lived with my mom, my grandmother Catherine, and my great-grandmother, Mamie.

"Brenda, don't you let him in that gate!" Mamie sternly shouted at my mother in her haste from the back of the house towards the front door.

Brenda stood on the front porch keeping a careful eye on me as I excitedly danced on the concrete walkway inside the gate, looking feverishly in both directions for the red Volkswagen Beetle in which my daddy would arrive. I can still remember the bubbly feeling that rested in my belly as I imagined the great time I was going to have just being with him. Maybe he would buy me something. Maybe he would take me someplace fun. I knew for sure he would pick me up, twirl me around, and hug me tight, and that was enough! Anything extra would be like Disney World. I remember my mother rolling her eyes upward so far in her head that only the white parts were visible.

"Grandmama, I'm standing on the porch. I'm not even at the gate! Brenda's tone was one of sharp, yet respectful agitation. "I'm grown! I'll open the gate for Robyn when Lawrence pulls up!"

"I don't want that boy inside this gate! This is my house and he ain't coming inside this gate! And I mean what I say!" Mamie's voice was angry and bitchy. And that is the way she translated to me all my life. Mean. Surly. Cantankerous. Agitated. Unreasonable. Difficult. A dejected tall, dark-skinned Black housekeeper for white folks, raising three children alone. Controlling *what* she could control. Controlling *who* she could control. Most everything else was outside of her control. Anything within the walls of the shotgun house at 740 Beach Street was within her control.

My mother didn't respond. She stood there, her right hand on her hip and her left arm across her midsection with her left hand gripping her right wrist. Seems like a weird posture, but my mother often stood that way when she was on the porch. It was almost as if the porch were a place where she could think—where she found peace enough to clear her head—and that was the position that gave her the most headspace for her time.

Around the corner of LaCaster Street onto the four hundred block of B Street came this streak of red, and I knew it was my daddy. I started screaming, jumping, and yelling, "Daddy, Daddy, Daddy!!"

"Robyn, Robyn! Wait till he gets in front of the house!" my mother said with a smile on her face and a sweetness in her voice. She started down the red steps towards the sidewalk where my little caramel-colored fingers were wrapped through, clutching the links in the dull silver-gray fence.

Brenda smiled in the direction of the car, with me jumping up and down between her and the fence. The red Volkswagen slowed and pulled close to the curb, and I could see him. His smile was so wide that it was clear from the driver's side window through the passenger's side window, like a ray of Florida sun. His teeth were pure white and short, like chicklets. There weren't any spaces between them, which made him seem all the more genuine, all the more dazzling.

He opened the door, and out came this smooth, debonaire, tall, handsome man. Had I been more than four years old, I would have said, oh good God, he's fine. But at four, all I knew to do was stare and grin and enjoy the pounding of my heart at the sight of him. This was the man of my dreams, and I was his girl. A daddy's girl.

Just as I knew he would, he picked me up and swung me around. I could feel the hot Florida summer breeze pick up the bottom of the pale-yellow dress I was wearing as it made a tent around my long, skinny legs. I could feel my long plats lift along with the bottom of my dress. I thought I was airborne. I screamed with excitement, bringing a very stern Mamie out of the house and onto the porch.

"Stop that gal from all that screaming! Makin' all that noise out here. All of that ain't necessary." At the sound of her voice, my plats returned to their original position and my dress bottom dropped as if someone had spanked it.

"Hey, Ms. Mamie. Hey, Ms. Catherine," said the handsome man still outside the gate.

"Hey, Lawrence," my grandmother returned his greeting. She was the dearest, kindest woman I knew.

"Don't come inside this gate, boy! And get from in front of my house," Mamie sharply retorted.

"Yes, ma'am. I'm going to be on my way in a minute," Lawrence nodded kindly, unable to impress Mamie. "Hey, Bren."

"Heyyyy…" my mother replied with a shy sexy smile.

He looked at her like she was a lollipop, and she returned a look that invited him to take a lick. It wouldn't be until later in my life that I would understand this exchange. He wanted to kiss her, and she wanted him to, but he dared not move any closer with Mamie's hawk eye glaring directly at him, her mouth prepared to embarrass my mother at the first sight of anything she could deem sinful. Lawrence put me in the car, and I happily waved bye to mother. And off the red Beetle chugged, making a right turn off Beach onto Bellevue Street. He looked over and smiled at me and said, *"You're so pretty."* I melted into the warm vinyl seat, feeling like the most beautiful and cherished girl anywhere.

Lawrence dropped me off back at Beech Street some hours later. I cannot remember specifically what we did together that day. I simply knew it was 'the best day ever,' as I described my good time to my mother. Most of the time I was around my dad, I was mesmerized by him. He had a flirtatious arrogant way of pulling everyone around him into the best of him. He was educated, and he taught himself to do many things. No one was as intelligent or as capable as he was to me. I felt that way even into my middle school years when I began spending several weeks of summer vacation with him in Jacksonville. My younger sister, Taran, and I would take the Greyhound from Pensacola to Jacksonville for an unspecified amount of our vacation. Lawrence would meet us on the platform, and from the sight of him waiting for us, I would jump up and down with my fingers gripping the links of the fence as I had done at four years old. Only now, I was older, and that excitement and the fence were contained on the inside.

Taran was vastly different from me. She was vibrant, not quite as serious, and had the cutest little round face that a little girl could have. Nothing and no one excited her that much. From an early age, she was content with herself. Her weak eyesight was hereditary—a malady passed down to her from Mamie. Behind her brown framed glasses was a precocious, curious girl that was comfortable enough with who she was to simply be who she was without apology. I was usually anxious, trying to please everyone around me. Somehow, and from somewhere, I learned to relish the approval of adults. I was respectful and given to politeness. Taran, although respectful and polite as well, was willing to challenge the flippant attitudes of some of the neighbors and family friends we knew as children. I admired that about her. I still do. That's how we were raised by the generations of women we lived with—to be polite and respectful—no matter the situation. No matter the insult. I breathed it in, snorted it like cocaine. Taran refused to be drugged by such irreverence. I wished I were her.

This was the time when children were to be seen and not heard, and when adults ruled. However, I am a master of language and language is meant to be heard. I talked early and could hold conversations with adults when I was very young. But I was told to be quiet. Catherine often said to me, "Hush up, girl! You talk too much! Learn to stay in your place." Her words were firm yet affirming. Unfortunately, this is not what I took away. I felt anything but affirmed. I took the posture of a doormat that read "step here." I was unaware that eventually, this posture would cripple me, causing me to accept as truth the harsh, critical rhetoric from some of those adults and every other person in my life. I wanted to please them more than myself. I wanted to be liked. I smiled through insults and laughed at jokes that were not funny, told at my expense. I wanted Mamie to like me, but she didn't. She thought I was too grown, too big for my britches. So, my progressive, protective mother put a pen and notebook in my hand and told me to write to keep me from talking and to try to keep Mamie off her warpath at the sound of my smart mouth. I learned to love written language. The apostle Paul in First Corinthians talks about God's provision of "a way of escape." Writing became mine.

Being the first grandchild and the first great-grandchild—adorable, precocious, and youthfully spiritual— I was expected to just smile and not respond, even if something felt bad to me. I would slither away with a smile on my face and cry to myself when no one was watching. Public school playground bullies perpetuated this type of shrinking. I wanted so desperately to be thought of as worthy. I received their insults with grace and cried in offense. I was always anxious about acquiring friends, and if I managed to make friends, I worked hard to keep them. I could be mouthy when it didn't work for me and silent when I should have spoken up. The constant feeling of being 'not right' and 'too much of one thing and not enough of the other' planted a seed of rejection that would be watered consistently by many water cans throughout my life. I hate the devil. His plans for us begin in the womb. Thankfully, so do the Lord's.

"You're so pretty," Lawrence said as soon as he saw me on the bus platform. The way he smiled at me was purely delightful. I melted once again.

He grabbed Taran and hugged her, and she giggled. "Taran Louise!" That was his nickname for her. She laughed and blushed, and I laughed and blushed because he made her as happy as he made me. That summer vacation was off to a fantastic start. The excitement of arriving in Jacksonville, heightened, because my stepsister, Marla, rode with my dad to pick us up. We never spoke to each other except on our summer visits, but we were always close as if there were no seasons in between.

Her maternal uncles had been unkind to her like mine had been to me, but in a different, more detrimental, and sinister way. My grandmother's brother, Jack, and my mother's brother, Lonnie, were intentionally churlish to me. They adored Taran but me, not so much. Again, they said I was *"too grown; too serious to be so young,"* and this was said within my hearing, directly to my face. I did not respond. I only cried. None of them ever touched me inappropriately, and I am grateful for that. Marla couldn't say the same.

She had sexual freedom that she gained from forces against her will. But it was freedom just the same. I was curious about it, and I wanted it. I coveted it. I wanted to be free. Marla openly shared her conquests with me, and I sat, listening intently as if I was hearing God speak. Some of it sounded too sensational to be true, as the stories of twelve and thirteen-year-old girls often are. Her stories were graphic. She was graphic. I couldn't wait to hear more, as I had come to like the feeling I felt at the base of my stomach when she talked. No one in my world talked about these kinds of things. Marla was putting meat on the bones of my imagination and without her knowledge. I was indebted to her for this.

The summer with Lawrence, his wife, Loretta, and Marla, was off to a great beginning. Plans were made to go to Sea World, St. Augustine, and Disney World. Lawrence and Loretta's daughter, Evette, the baby sister of the group, would make these excursions so much fun. She was a mystery to me. I was introduced to her in the most peculiar way. She seemed to be a secret I wasn't supposed to be privy to. Evette was around six years old and brighter in skin tone than Marla. Although they shared the same mom, they looked nothing alike. Evette was more the color of margarine than butter. She had short red hair and reminded me of a vintage Raggedy Ann doll. She was always flexible and playful but given more responsibility than a girl her age should have. She did dishes, vacuumed floors, cleaned the bathroom, ironed her clothes, and was learning how to cook. Most of these duties were assigned by Marla, who was laden with household chores as punishment for her consistent disobedience—which is how she exercised a part of her freedom. Tara and I were overwhelmed by such work. While we had small chores, my mother's priority was our education since she had been the first to graduate college in our family. There was never a question of *whether* we were going to college; it was simply a question of *where* we were going to college. Marla and Evette didn't seem to be on the college track. They were being groomed to take care of a man, and Lawrence made it clear that this was his goal for them, and that my mother was crazy because she didn't have us on the same life track. Once I got to know her, I loved Evette, and I enjoyed the fun of having another little sister.

We never made it to Sea World or Disney World. We never made it anywhere fun that summer. All we did was stay in the house while my father and stepmother worked. We couldn't go outside, except for right in front of the house, or across the street to Marla and Evette's grandmother's house. The house had to be cleaned, the dinner had to be prepared, and this is what we did all summer—day after day, week after week. At the beginning of each week, I was hopeful that my dad would take us to do something fun, as he promised my mother he would. But he was always busy, always given to what was important to him, which didn't seem to be hanging out with his kids. Keeping house was the summer fun and I felt cheated and angry, but unable to say so. The highlight of the days for me became my father coming home from work. I assumed that he would greet me the same way he did at the fence or on the bus platform. I soon faced abrupt disappointment.

I learned quickly that my father's arrival home was nothing short of unsettling for everyone in the house. Marla and Evette would scurry at the sound of his Chevy Impala's turn into the carport. Soon, Taran and I were doing the same. We ran around making sure nothing was out of place and that the obvious things that he told us to do were completed, at least on the surface. The jingling of his keys was like a warden's at bed check. Because I was only visiting, I always attempted to greet him with excitement, which was often met with a dry hello, his thin lips pursed tightly to near invisibility. That meant to leave him alone. I would retreat in fear, internalizing whatever negative assessment he would make of the day's chores or us personally. One person he always smiled upon seeing was Marla. No matter his mood, he always addressed her with pleasure.

"Hey, Shugg!" he greeted her.

"Hey, Shugg!" Marla returned the greeting. This was his nickname for her and hers for him. He had no nickname for me. He occasionally, in a light moment, would call me "Robbie" and that became a moment of relaxation for me. But I didn't consider it a nickname. If a person gives another a nickname, it communicates a special endearment that the formal name bypasses. Shugg was short for Sugar. Even their nickname for each other had a nick-name, a further indication of my being bypassed by my king.

On the coffee table in the living room was a marble chessboard. Ivory-colored marble replaced the white pieces and caramel-colored marble represented the black side. One day, my father arrived home with his lips tucked inside his teeth and immediately went to the chessboard. He was sipping a pint of Johnny Walker Red out of the bottle and chasing it with a Miller Genuine Draft.

"Robyn," he called to me. Taran, Evette, and I had already scattered at his entrance, and the call of my formal name indicated a complication. I knew better than to verbally respond. I moved my feet and landed next to his chair.

"Yes, Daddy?"

"Do you know how to play chess?

"Uhhh…no."

"I want you to learn how to play chess while you're here. You need to know the strategy. You need to know how to win."

"OK, Daddy!" Anything to please him and be released before this went badly. I started back towards the other end of the house, like a flash.

"Robyn. I wasn't finished talking to you."

My stomach dropped. I pivoted and returned to his side, "Yes, Daddy."

"I want you to read this book by the time I get home from work tomorrow."

It was an 8x11 paperback titled *How to Master the Art of Chess*. My stomach dropped even further. As if not having a true nickname wasn't enough pain, this gift of a book to finish in a day was an indication that this man didn't know me at all. All he knew was that I was pretty. He had no idea that I had difficulty with reading comprehension, or he would have never expected me to read anything in a day, not to mention being able to implement what it said.

He continued, "If you don't read it, I'm going to think you're stupid."

He handed me the book. I took it back to the bedroom and put it on the dresser without saying a word. But I didn't cry. For the first time, I permitted myself not to like him. I permitted myself to be angry that he lived in an opulent house with Loretta and her three children, two of whom were not biologically his, while Taran and I watched our mother struggle to make ends meet. Sometimes without lights. Sometimes without gas. Sometimes without water. Sometimes without two of these at the same time. I fully allowed myself to hate him because he didn't care enough about me to provide for me. He had stacks of money that he bragged about and threw around, but he never threw any of it my way. And this had nothing to with brat-like wants that many young girls pester their fathers for. My basic needs suffered from his selfishness. He never had a reason for not providing for us. I would discover in adulthood that he was selfish by his admission and proud to be so. Mean. Sociopathic. Emotionally complicated. Unreasonable. Alcoholic. Damaged. By the time he handed me that chess book with the premeditated decision to find me stupid if I didn't read it, my fingers let go of the links in the fence, and I replaced the transparent fence with a high wall of shiplap and black paint. However, I left millimeter-sized spaces between the boards just in case he decided to be different. He never did.

We returned to Jacksonville for our extended summer visit for the next several years. Each summer would begin with "you're so pretty" and end with some cruel, unwarranted, belittling criticism from my father. The summer before I turned sixteen would be the final time that I'd give my summertime to him, only to carry out punitive consequences for Marla's misbehavior. It was the last time I willingly put myself in my father's presence for an undetermined duration, to be pretty at the beginning of the day, only to be pretty rejected at the end.

Today, in an ever-evolving society where a Black woman is a queen, Black Girl Magic is familiar, and we have chosen to celebrate ourselves no matter our complexion or size. One would think that being raised in a house full of women would have been somewhat of a pre-generational celebration of modern-day girl power. My life in the house on Beach Street offered a much greater complexity than that. A world where men were absent, considered dangerous, and discussed as if not trustworthy but bowed to when they were present, is confusing for a growing girl. The mistreatment I received from my father and uncles underscored the confusion I experienced, which had turned to trepidation. When I should have learned how to relate to men, I was gripped with a ruinous, immobilizing fear and a curious uncertainty about them. The women I lived with, held to an unspoken religious ideology that the adoration of men meant you were fast—wayward and untoward in some fashion. Mamie shamefully punished Brenda for being that way because she had a baby out of wedlock with a fast-talking Negro from a few streets up. Mamie's behavior towards Brenda dulled the bright light over the house on Beach Street. Mamie was an elder in her Primitive Baptist church. She was looked up to and revered for the woman of God she was. And there was Brenda, her granddaughter, who changed the air from holy to whorish. As a result, I came forth in shame and rejection. I hate the devil. His plan is at work from the womb. Thankfully, so is the Lord's.

They never talked about men or a desire for them. I never heard them reminisce about their weddings or brag about how fine they once were and how they couldn't keep the men away like most women begin to do in their 50s and 60s. Any talk of romance or a love interest was treated like a dirty little secret—like the mention of it would create the atmospheric condition of whoredom. I remember the moment I discovered that my mother was so much more than my mother; she was a *woman*. Being a woman and being cognizant of my womanly desires, I understand she had hers. Sexual desires. I was angry that she never talked to me about them, that she never let me in on the fact that she wasn't asexual like the women who raised her, and helped to raise me, presented themselves to be. I was angry that the man next door that I thought was just a man who was nice to us was really her boyfriend. I wondered why she never presented him as such, why he never had dinner with us, why she was affectionate with him in front of us. I could have benefited greatly from that. It was easy to forgive her when I recognized that she was a product of her environment and all she could teach me was what she had learned. We were flowers grown in the same garden.

That was an unimaginable state of confusion to live in. I was so desperate to be liked by men, that I kissed my first boy at age ten. I let several boys put their hands under my plaid private school uniform, so as not to feel left out of what other girls were experiencing. It was fun to keep that a secret from the protective women I was with at home. A predominantly white parochial school limited my chances of meeting anyone in high school. A distant cousin, a fact unknown to me while we were dating, was my date for the senior prom. I couldn't wait to get to college. I would meet the man of my dreams—a tall Black man, educated, sexy, mysterious, and able to do almost anything. He would love me at first sight. He would embrace all of me, even the confusing parts that I didn't understand about myself. I would be uninhibited. Free, like Marla.

I had designed the blueprint for how I'd become intimate with this replacement king. However, the exact opposite happened. The fear of men I carried left me open to exchange the replacement king with queens. This story calls for a chapter of its own. My decision to leave out the details is acceptable because I have nothing to hide or explain. I am no longer ashamed or diminished by the experiences of the past. I have dealt with God face-to-face, wrestled with Him as Jacob did, faced all my imps, and I have the limp to prove it. I still believe that He will bless me with the Godly man of my dreams, with a loving relationship that will carry me into my latter years with extreme joy.

Sexually repressed Christian women annoyed me until I recognized that I was unintentionally bred to be one of them. I lived a sexually free experience in my head that I was unable to actualize in real-time. I was pure—chaste—until 47 years old. That may sound pious and quite holy until the skirt is lifted and one discovers that there's more to the inflexibility of those starched white panties than the willpower to avoid fornication. There are armed guards that keep our intimate places of entry intact, even barricaded. I know, experientially, that those keepers of the gate are fear and shame, rather than an unrelenting devotion to the Father, which makes virginity after a certain age, overrated. Too much weight as a measure of virtuous living is given to it in the Christian woman's life.

Dr. King said longevity has its place, as does virginity, I suppose. But Dr. King didn't experience longevity, and I wonder if the denial of sexual experience and the expression of its pleasure is as much a premature loss as Dr. King's life came to be. Some of my readers will think of this as sacrilege and I'm comfortable with that. It begs deeper conversation and exploration, and I welcome that. Consciously, I've not known a woman who preserved herself for that long to be any holier or more inclined towards Divine blessings than the ladies who uncovered their entryways earlier, and often. The only thing those ladies had that a woman like me didn't have was more fun.

Who knows? Maybe had my dad not been such a source of fear for me, I would have been brave enough to be open myself to the advances of men much earlier. Somewhere in my shadowed head-spaces, I thought I was undesirable to men, that I was unpleasant in every way. That's how Lawrence made me feel: unpleasant and unacceptable. Rejected. I wasn't "that girl"—the girl who made all the boys turn and pay attention when she entered the room. Marla was "that girl." Even Taran and Evette were "those girls." But not me. Every man in my life had been a confirmation of this, including the man I finally gave myself to and then married. The short length of that union gave me the courage to ask my father some critical questions I desperately wanted answers to. But time and illness stole my courage, and before I knew it, he was dead at sixty-eight years old.

There he lay… the handsome man that picked me up at the fence and whisked me away in the red Beetle. How he suffered in his final moments. Days earlier, brown urine, the consistency and color of chocolate milk, hung in a bag beside his bed. I watched his face sunken in from the damage to his liver and the toxins that ravaged his body from a life of alcoholism. And how peaceful he looked lying there in his dark, charcoal suit. Fine and debonaire as he'd always been. Lord have mercy!! The funeral director worked miracles with his face. Standing there, I hung on to his accomplishments, still wishing he loved me as much as I loved him—still a daddy's girl.

On his death bed, my father's final words to me were spoken to his wife, in front of me, like I wasn't there, "Make sure she doesn't get any of my money." I had just finished wiping a mess from his naked behind when he spit those words. For a moment, the feelings I had about the chess book returned, and an angry heat ascended from my belly towards the top of my head. Tears welled in my eyes, but I dried them quickly. I remembered that I'd already forgiven this man, that I had made peace with who he was, and that he was incapable of being the daddy I so desperately wanted.

I didn't need to revisit that pain because I had a father—the *Father*—who found me not only loving but *lovable*. He has always been my Provider. He has always been my Rock. He is never absent. Never abdicating. Never abusive. I have a Father who I could call Daddy, and He behaves like one. That dying skeleton missed out on the greatest blessing of his life—having *me* for a daughter. He missed out on my unconditional love for him. He missed out on Taran. He missed out on Evette. I wrote his obituary, and I honored him. I spoke about him, and I honored him. I interred him, and I honored him. The tears I cried were not those of pain and heartache, nor those of guilt or regret. They were tears of victory because I learned to love someone incapable of loving me back. Unconditional love is love in its purest form. I am open and ready to accept a real partner because I'm healed from needing a daddy. I have one who is eternally and completely mine. He whispers daily to me, *"You're so pretty."* And I trust Him.

Acceptance is an *internal* decision that forces us to echo that decision *externally*. I am unconditionally and unapologetically *me*. I have learned to accept words with grace, compliments, accolades, and wisdom. I have also learned to accept with humility, constructive criticism while sifting through negativity and brutishness. For to be gracious is not to be a silent welcome mat for violence. It is the reclaimed version of "speak when you're spoken to, come when you're called." Grace is practiced in quiet strength. Quiet strength has carried me from being *pretty rejected* to *perfectly accepted*.

ABOUT THE AUTHOR

 Robyn Rease is the founder and artistic director of *Stage Praise Productions,* a theatre, film, and television company whose mission is to change the face of entertainment—and the world—one story at a time! Writing since childhood, Robyn is a prolific poet, playwright, short storyteller, screenwriter, and minister. She has written countless collections of poetry and has written more than a hundred skits and full-length plays, directing and producing nearly 40 of them at different churches and venues all along the east coast.

Robyn was the director of a church theatre company for more than 12 years. In 2007, she developed *Empty Kitchen Chairs* for the screen and shot the trailer for the feature-length film along with Centurion Filmworks. Her video of the stage play, *Beyond Grace* (formerly *Show Me the Glory*), was acquired and nationally distributed by Maverick Entertainment and can be found on Tubi, IMBd, and Amazon Prime Video.

After 25 years of service in the public school system, Robyn is a retired middle school administrator. Recently, she started her own writing business, *PENsive Professional & Creative Writing Services* where she writes both technically and creatively. She also teaches writing and English conventions to students and adult learners. Robyn lives in Durham, North Carolina.

CHAPTER 7

Adoption: "Mr. Will" Saved My Life

by Sandra James

"Start children off on the way they should go, and even when they are old they will not turn from it." Proverbs 22:6 (NIV)

This little black girl is a Coal Miner's daughter. Blacks worked the mines back in those days, but we were called Negroes. My birth certificate says Negro. When they came out of the mines, they all looked the same—black. My sister and I were adopted by a man named Will Henry, and we called him "Mr. Will." I know an old man with no wife adopting two baby girls at birth sounds unbelievable. We lived in the house with my great aunt

Gladys and great uncle Whit. Mr. Will lived across the railroad tracks. Every morning Mr. Will came across the railroad tracks to our house for breakfast. They were old, so my sister and I did a lot of the grown-up stuff; shopping and paying bills. We grew up fast but had a great life in the hills of West Virginia. I remember going to church all the time, and the pastor came to our house on Sundays for dinner. This is where I got my foundation, where I learned about God and that church, family, and community are everything.

As a kid in West Virginia, I worried about nothing because we had everything: house, chickens, hogs, pigs, and we grew fruits and vegetables. When we slaughtered a hog or pig, there was food for all the neighbors. No one went hungry or without. If we wanted something from the store, all my sister and I had to do was sign Mr. Will's name with an "X." They could not read or write, but they paid the bill each month. We did not have running water or a bathroom, but you do not miss what you never had.

There are always those big moments in life that change your life forever. I slept in the bed with Aunt Gladys, and one morning when I woke up, she was cold. I thought it was odd that she was still sleeping because, in West Virginia, we got up with the chickens. I put some covers on her and went back to sleep. When I woke up again, she was still sleeping and even colder. I shook her and started yelling her name, "Aunt Gladys, Aunt Gladys, wake up, wake up," but she didn't get up. I knew something was wrong and went and got Uncle Whit. My aunt Gladys was dead.

I was not afraid because it was customary that when someone died, the viewing of the body was in your house, in the living room. I remember our neighbor next door, Grover, we called him, died, but he still used to come to visit us. The front screen door would open and close (we never locked our doors), the radio would turn on, and the rocking chair would start rocking. Aunt Gladys would say, "Oh, that is just Grover coming to visit." So, death was just a normal part of life for us. As a kid, I did not worry about anything; things were just the way it was, nothing more, nothing less.

After Aunt Gladys died, my sister and I took care of Uncle Whit and Mr. Will, with the help of the neighbors, of course. We were probably around six and eight years old. We knew our birth mother. She, our stepfather, and two brothers came to visit during the summertime when school was out, or we visited them in Rochester, New York. As I think about it now, I wonder why my mother did not come to get us after Aunt Gladys died. A few years later, Mr. Will died of black lung. He was a cold miner, and it was not too long after that when someone called child protective services, and my mother came and moved us to Rochester.

After Mr. Will died, my sister and I got two checks, social security, and black lung. He also had enough money saved in the bank to take good care of us. The bank account was in our names, but we lived in the country where they took your handshake as your word. So, my mother got us, all the money in the bank and four checks each month. Now, she had a reason to come get us.

However, as it is written: "What no eye has seen, what no ear has heard, and what no human mind has conceived"— the things God has prepared for those who love him—1 Corinthians 2:9

We moved to the big city of Rochester. Well, it was big to me. In West Virginia, life was like it is in the movies I watch now. Blacks and whites did not live, play, or go to the same school. I had a lot of fun with my brothers. I was what you call a tomboy. We played basketball, football, we boxed. My mother used to say I was fast because I was always with the boys. I was told to keep my dress down and panties up. I did not wear dresses and did not know what that meant. I was just one of the boys. A couple of movies that come to mind that describe the life I had living with my mother are *Cinderella* and *Precious*.

My sister and I became the live-in maids. We cleaned the house and washed and ironed everyone's clothes. I remember putting creases in the pillowcases and the handkerchiefs. I could hear the other kids outside playing while we did everything except cooking, including making their bed. I know this sounds crazy, but I was told as a kid that I was a whore because I did not know who my father was, and I still do not know. Yeah, and I was a bald-headed b***h too. I have that thick, coarse hair, and my mother (part Indian) has straight "good hair," so they call it.

My stepfather was a good man. He worked hard, did the grocery shopping, and did most of the cooking. He was the peacemaker in the family, and everyone loved him. We felt safe and taken care of. But sometimes, the very one that saves you can hurt you too. My sister and I slept in the same bed. I slept on the other side by the window, away from the door. I would hear his footsteps and lay there praying that he would stop on her side and not come over to my side of the bed at night. We never talked about what happened at night when he would come into the room, but his hands found their way under the covers and rubbed between our legs. We knew it was wrong, but we had to protect the only person that protected us from our mother. Remember, I was the whore that didn't know who her daddy was. Oh yeah, and the bald-headed b***h.

When I was about 14 years old, I used to think of ways to kill my mother. I hated her. I blamed her for everything. Surely, with her room right across the hall, she had to know what was happening to us, and she did nothing. After a few years of running away and being brought back home, I was finally put into juvenile jail. When I appeared in front of the judge, he said, "Why are you here? You do not have a record or have been in trouble before. Do you have someone that can come get you?" I was not prepared for that question. I thought I would be placed in a home until I turned 18. My mind raced. Who would come to get me and take care of me? I said, "My uncle's girlfriend might come, not the wife but the girlfriend." I gave the judge her name and phone number, and he went into his chambers and called her. She came, and he released me to her care. If I had never seen God work before, I did right there. God and all my angels (Aunt Gladys, Uncle Whit, and Mr. Will) spoke to the judge that day on my behalf.

> *"And we know that in all things God works for the good of those who love him, who[a] have been called according to his purpose." Romans 8:28*

Come with me now, to another life-changing moment. I had lived in West Virginia, segregated, and then Rochester. Now I was living in Webster, New York, with a white foster mother, and you could count the number of Blacks who lived there on one hand, maybe two, counting my new siblings and me. Life was good. But you know that saying, you can take the girl out the city but not the city out the girl? I was in the city whenever I had the chance, thinking I was missing something.

One day, I overheard my foster mother talking on the phone about moving to Seattle, Washington, with her brother. I had never met her brother and definitely did not want to move with them, so I got an apartment in the city. How was that possible? I was able to get an apartment because I was receiving two checks a month (social security and black lung). I could not enroll myself in high school because I was only 16 and did not have an adult to register me.

They were gone for about a year, and during this time, I met Ramon, "Ricky," my first love. Things didn't work out in Seattle, so my foster family (mother, brothers, sister) moved back to Webster. My foster mother let us move in with them so that I could finish school. I was pregnant, and it was my senior year of High School. Oh, did I tell you Ricky was Puerto Rican, fine as wine, with "good hair," so I knew my babies wouldn't have hair like mine—you know, that "bad hair."

Shortly after my daughter was born, we moved back to the city, and a year later, daughter number two was born. Life was not easy; 19 years old with two babies. I knew, in my heart, that this was not the life God wanted for me. There had to be more.

I had a job and would drop the girls off at daycare and take the bus to work. There was never any money left after paying the bills and daycare. One morning on the way to work, something (Holy Spirit) told me to join the Army. I went to the payphone booth, called in sick, to work and walked into the recruiting office to join the Army. I had not talked this over with anyone.

I just knew this was the right path to take. I had no idea who would keep the girls or how this would all play out. I just knew I had to leave to live.

Of all the people in my life, who do you think kept my girls for me while I went to Basic Training and Advanced Individual Training (AIT)? My birth mother kept them. I know you are probably thinking, how could I leave them with her? I was more afraid to leave them with his mother because my girls were her only grandchildren at the time, and she would have fought me for custody. It was a sacrifice to leave them, but I did this so that we could have a better life.

After Basic Training, I went to my first duty station in Germany. I was scared. I could not imagine what it would be like to live in another country. God knew what He was doing, but I didn't. Remember, my Christian life was back in West Virginia when I was a little girl. All those years later, I was trying to stand on everything I remembered…that God would see me through. When I got to Germany, they tried to kick me out for fraudulent enlistment because I did not give up custody of my girls, and was trying to bring them to Germany. I stood on the Word of God. I knew that if God told me to join the military, there would be nothing they could do about it. No one understood why I wasn't nervous. But when God puts it in your heart, you stand, have faith, and trust. And I stood on the rock. What other choice did I have? I'm so glad I did—God saw me through 20 years in the military. I raised my two daughters and retired in January 2007. It was the best decision, and I am truly thankful that I obeyed the voice of God.

"My sheep listen to my voice; I know them, and they follow me." John 10:27

I was just a kid (19 years old) raising two girls by myself. We grew up together, my girls and me. I stayed with their father much longer (seven years) than I should have. My mission in life was that they would have and know their father, no matter the cost (mental and physical abuse). I wanted them to have what I didn't have—a father. A girl can only take so much. My self-esteem was very low. When you are told for so long that you are nothing, after a while, you start to believe it. I tried several times to leave him but would always take him back. The bond, the soul tie when you have children with someone, is like a drug. I just kept going back to him. One time I left him, and he came by my apartment to see the girls. My guy friend's car was parked outside. He was so mad that he shot up the car with the guy sitting in it. Thankfully, no one was hurt. We made the news.

Joining the military, and being sent to Germany, saved my life. This was my final break, my drug rehabilitation, my freedom.

Throughout every duty station from Germany-Georgia-Korea-Japan-Texas-Washington and back to Korea, God always placed someone in my life to guide, mentor, and help me along the way (angels). I was an angry Black woman, mad at the world, and God knew that I could not live holding onto that hate.

Let me tell you about my mountain top experience. I was invited by a fellow soldier to a Christian retreat, Tres Dias (three days). I laughed. Who me, going on a retreat with a bunch of church folks? Thanks, but no, thank you. I didn't want to be around church folks, not my idea of fun. I was having too much fun in the world.

While in the military, I worked during evenings at the Non-commissioned Officer (NCO) Club as a waitress/bartender. I was having the time of my life. Men looked at me and thought I was beautiful, and I got a lot of attention. Also, I made a lot of money in tips. I was the only Black female waitress/bartender at the club. That soldier just kept inviting me, and one day I said OK. Tres Dias was a three-day retreat with God. No watch, no cell phone, no outside communication. Just time with God without any distractions. This was the beginning of my relationship with God. It took Him getting me to another country to lead me to the mountain top to spend time with Him—to know Him for myself.

After that wonderful experience, I kept bartending, telling myself that God understood because I needed the money to care for my girls. I started going to church, where I was an usher, but I was still working at the club. I began to feel like the hypocrite that I thought the church folks were before my mountain top experience. One day in church, I asked God to show himself to me. I needed to know Him for real, for real. I tried Him, I asked him to take smoking cigarettes away from me, and He did just that. He took the desire from me. From that day on, I have not smoked anything. The chaplain would also come by my office and talk regularly. He never tried to beat me over the head with the Bible, telling me I was going to Hell for working at the club. He just kept coming by, showing love. Little did I know that he was watering the seed, and it was growing inside of me. I cannot lie and say I was an angel from this day forward, but this was the beginning of my Christian walk.

"I planted the seed, Apollos watered it, but God has been making it grow. So, neither the one who plants nor the one who waters are anything, but only God, who makes things grow. The one who plants and the one who waters have one purpose, and they will each be rewarded according to their labor." 1 Corinthians 3:6-8

Not knowing who my father was/is, caused me to look for love in all the wrong places and faces. I was searching, trying to fill that void. I desperately wanted to have a loving, caring family. My girls love me unconditionally, but there was still something missing. I received an invite to join the Order of Eastern Stars (female Masons), a Bible-based organization that does charity work. Usually, to join, you must be in the bloodline of a relative. However, it was open, and I was honored to join. I soon learned it is a secret society that takes care of its own. One can get a job or promotion purely on a handshake. It felt so good to belong, be cared for, looked out for, and protected from the world. If you are traveling as a Mason, there is nothing you need to be afraid of. I was stranded at the airport in another country because my flight was delayed. However, I wore the light symbol on my jacket, and a fellow brother took me home, and his wife and friends treated me like family. If your car breaks down on the highway and you have the emblems on your car, one of your brothers will stop to help, and you do not fear going with a stranger because he is your brother. This is how we should treat one another as Christians. We went on a trip, and we all cooked food. A guy sitting at the back of the bus asked me for a piece of chicken, but I was told not to give it to him if he was traveling (Mason). They take care of their own. I wanted to take care of everyone. I thought it was Bible-based because of the offices within the organization: Chaplain, Ruth, Ester, etc. There were many ministers, deacons, and deaconesses, within the church that held offices in the organization.

However, God began to open my eyes to see that this was not of Him. I was the secretary, and we were taking a class through induction, and suddenly, I was not in that room anymore. I saw a vision of white clothes, lamps, and women walking like in a labyrinth in a devil-worshiping movie. It scared me as I knew this was a vision from God to let me know this was not my path. I was afraid because I was a babe in Christ, so who was I to tell those more knowledgeable than me what God showed me. I went to my chaplain for advice. He told me, either you please God or man, but you cannot please both. Of course, when I told them I was leaving, I was made to feel like I was crazy and did not know what I was talking about. Why would God show me something He did not show or tell them? After all, they were ministers and knew the Word better than me. I know what I saw and felt. That was enough for me.

The obstacle that prevents us from wise investment is the heart. Wherever our treasure is, there will our hearts be (Matthew 6:21). We follow what captivates our hearts, and Jesus made it clear that we cannot serve two masters. A master is anything that enslaves us. Alcohol, lust, and money are all masters of some people. Jesus calls us to follow Him and abandon all other masters. Sometimes you must stand alone, even when others do not understand. I had to trust God on this one. The flesh did not want to leave because it was fun, belonging, being a part of an organization, that others look up to and bow down to.

"No one can serve two masters. Either he will hate the one and love the other, or you will be devoted to the one and despise the other. You cannot serve both God and money." Matthew 6:24

The enemy, the devil, has his way of making you feel alone, and I allowed it. After being around people at work and church, and after the kids went to bed, there was this overwhelming feeling of being alone and that no one cared or loved me. This caused me to lie in bed, having one big pity party, feeling sorry for myself. I was going to work and church with a big smile like everything was alright. Inside, I was hurting, feeling abandoned, and thrown away.

Until one day, I got fed up with letting life, people, and myself, just beat me down. Every relationship ended in abuse—mental and physical. Until I cried out to God as Job did in Job, Chapter 10. God will not and did not join me in my pity party. He came when I finally cried out that I could not do this on my own and needed Him to show up in my life. He did just that. He used a female minister at my church who was preparing for an upcoming women's conference to ask me to dance. I said, "You must be mistaken, I'm not the dance leader." She replied, "God told me, you and me; said you must have heard him wrong." God then made me remember that I often repeated what the pastor said. "Lord, I will go where you want me to go, I will say what you want me to say, and I will do what you want me to do." But I had no idea that He would ask me to praise dance. I agreed, and we started practicing. The minister chose the song, brought the dress, and taught me the choreography.

I was like a little kid, learning something entirely new, and I looked like a fish out of water. Remember that I was a tomboy who played basketball, football, and boxed? I did not dance. Can you imagine how scared I was? That was when I began to fully trust God—you know, that blind kind of faith. I made a deal with God. If this is what you want me to do, we will do it together. My part was to practice and just show up, and He had to do the rest.

My game plan was to go up to the front of the conference room, put my head down, hands in prayer position, and not move until He moved. I stayed in the bathroom until it was time to come out. I had on a peach gown bought from a used clothing store, a white leotard, white palazzo pants, and white gloves. I was so scared, but I trusted that it was God's voice she heard. I wish it was recorded on video because I do not remember anything, except I was battling in the spirit. I had never had this type of experience before. The dance ministry leader was upset because I was asked to dance at the conference. She called our pastor to stop it because she had not approved it, and when he didn't, she came to the conference dressed in all black and sat in the back row. This was my first experience of truly going to war with the enemy. This was the beginning of the ministry of dance God birthed in me. You know the saying, "Be careful what you ask for, or you just might get it." I did not ask for dance, but I asked God many times about what my gifts were and what my purpose was. I used to stand at the door as an usher, watching others preaching, singing, and using their gifts. I just knew surely, there had to be something for me. I have always wished I had a voice to sing, but dance, God? He really does have a sense of humor.

"Direct my footsteps according to your word; let no sin rule over me." Psalm 119:133

On New Year's Eve 2004, our pastor told us to write down our vision for 2005 and put it in our bibles, not a New Year's resolution, but a declaration. To write your vision as in *Habakkuk 2:2: "Write down the revelation and make it plain on tablets, so that a herald may run with it. For the revelation awaits an appointed time; it speaks of the end and will not prove false. Though it lingers, wait for it; it will certainly come and will not delay."* I wrote I would get married in 2005.

I started telling my family and friends that I was getting married that year. The question was, who are you dating? And the answer was, no one, but I am getting married this year. I told enough people and said it enough that I began to believe it. I did not know who or when, but I was standing on that it would happen that year, 2005. I'm here to tell you that I got married in December 2005.

Our dating occurred over the phone. I went to Korea in September 2005, and we had a long-distance relationship from September until December. We got married on December 4, 2005, in Washington State, where we met. It all seemed so unreal, but it was God-ordained. When I met my husband a few years prior, he was married, sang in the choir at church, and we had mutual friends. I remember we went to a leadership conference in Texas with our pastor and everyone was trying to hook up the single lady with the single minister who just so happened to be his roommate on the trip. His wife died in May 2005. I would call and check on how he was doing, and we would laugh and talk about the conference. He teased me that I would never get married because I was looking for Mr. Perfect. As a joke, when I called and got his voicemail, I would say, "Hey, this is Sandra, looking for my Mr. Perfect," and he became my Mr. Perfect. It's so unreal how it all happened. His first wife's family—mother, sisters, and nieces—all came to the wedding, and there was no drama, only love, and peace. It still amazes me that God loves me so much that He gave me the desires of my heart. It has been 16 years, and we are still happily married. He is the man God chose for me, and he loves him some Sandra.

I am in awe every day of the things God has done for this little Black girl from West Virginia. I am so thankful that I was obedient and did as I told God that I would—go, do, and say whatever He wanted me to do. Because of one dance, years ago, God sent me on mission trips to South Africa, Haiti, Jamaica, Belize, Dominican Republic, and Costa Rica, showing His love through dance. Had I not accepted that dance, I would still be searching for my purpose.

My prayer for you is to listen to that voice within and do not worry about what others might think. Show the world that there is nothing too hard for God.

I no longer look for love in all the wrong places. God has filled that void with His love. I'm so very grateful that I have a Father, God. I believe every Word in the Bible to be true. My adoption saved my life. Had it not been for my life in West Virginia, I would not have been trained as a child. I lost my way but found my way back to Him. It is still hard for me to believe how far God has brought me and how He has surrounded me with so much love from family and friends. I am His favorite: beautiful, number one.

"Then I heard the voice of the Lord saying, "Whom shall I send? And who will go for us?" And I said, "Here am I. Send me!" *Isaiah 6:8*

ABOUT THE AUTHOR

SFC Sandra Kay James, USA, Ret., is a Chaplain and a Minister of Word and Dance. She ministers in dance every Sunday in her local church and at a Shelter for the homeless. She also serves in the Missions and Outreach Ministry. Sandra ministers in dance throughout her community, conferences, and Missions trips to Haiti, Belize, Jamaica, Costa Rica, Dominican Republic, and South Africa. She has a heart for God's people. God used others to reach her, and she desires to do the same by showing God's love through Word and Dance.

Sandra retired from the United States Army in 2007 with 20 years of service. She has a Bachelor of Arts and Business Management degree from the University of Maryland, a Master of Arts degree in Biblical Studies, and a Master of Divinity degree from Beulah Heights University, Licensed in Word and Dance (2017) from Eagles International Training Institute (EITI).

She resides in Georgia with her amazing husband, Raymond. They have four children and seven grandchildren.

Made in the USA
Columbia, SC
19 April 2022

59164889R00070